THE MEDIEVAL CANON LAW

Knowledge of the canon law was essential for the medieval ecclesiastical administrator, and teaching in canon law was provided in all western universities in the Middle Ages.

This study examines the provision for students (especially in Cambridge), the choice of available textbooks, and the collections of legal books made by the university and colleges and by private individuals.

Official teaching of canon law ceased at the Reformation, but the study continued in the faculties of civil law; medieval texts were reissued and many new guides to the current practice of church courts written.

THE
MEDIEVAL CANON LAW

TEACHING, LITERATURE AND TRANSMISSION

DOROTHY M. OWEN

Emeritus Keeper,
Cambridge University Archives

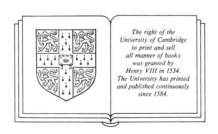

The right of the
University of Cambridge
to print and sell
all manner of books
was granted by
Henry VIII in 1534.
The University has printed
and published continuously
since 1584.

CAMBRIDGE UNIVERSITY PRESS

Cambridge
New York   Port Chester
Melbourne   Sydney

Published by the Press Syndicate of the University of Cambridge
The Pitt Building, Trumpington Street, Cambridge CB2 IRP
40 West 20th Street, New York, NY 10011, USA
10 Stamford Road, Oakleigh, Melbourne 3166, Australia

First published 1990

Printed in Great Britain at
the University Press, Cambridge

British Library cataloguing in publication data
Owen, Dorothy M. (Dorothy Mary), *1920*
The medieval canon law.
1. England. Christian church. Canon law, history
I. Title   II. Series
262.90942

Library of Congress cataloguing in publication data
Owen, Dorothy Mary.
The medieval canon law: teaching, literature, and
transmission/ Dorothy M. Owen.
p.   cm. – (Sandars lectures in bibliography: 1987–1988)
Includes bibliographical references.
ISBN 0 521 39313 2
1. Canon law – Study and teaching – Europe – History.
2. Canonists – Europe.   3. Canon law – Bibliography.
I. Title.   II. Series.
LAW
262.9'2'07 – dc20   90–32480   CIP

ISBN 0 521 39313 2 hardback

CRC

In Memory

Contents

List of figures

Preface

WITHOUT THE ENCOURAGEMENT offered by my election to the Sandars readership in bibliography I could never have contemplated the composition of these lectures, and I am deeply grateful to the electors for the honour they did me. I should never have decided on this topic without the training I received at Manchester from Christopher Cheney more than forty years ago, and without the encouragement of his friendship, which continued uninterrupted until his death two years ago. I have other debts to acknowledge, however: to Joan Varley and Kathleen Major who introduced me to the canon law in action at Lincoln, to successive bishops of Ely and librarians of the University Library who encouraged me to exploit the ecclesiastical materials for which I was, and still am, responsible, and to my fellow students of medieval church courts and canon lawyers, Donald Logan, Richard Helmholz, James Brundage, Jane Sayers, Charles Donahue, and David Smith, with whom I have discussed some at least of what I have said here and from whose friendship I have greatly profited. My colleagues in the University Library, and especially Elisabeth Leedham-Green, and a number of my students, have assisted the searches I have needed to make. Some of my fellow archivists and librarians outside Cambridge have helped me to uncover material. Most of all I am, as always, grateful for the tolerance and encouragement of my husband, who has lived with these and related topics since 1958.

What I have done here is not more than a scraping of the surface: I hope that it will encourage other scholars to dig much more deeply.

Abbreviations

BIHR	*Bulletin of the Institute of Historical Research*
BL	British Library
BRUC	A.B. Emden, *Biographical Register of the University of Cambridge*, Cambridge 1963
BRUO	A.B. Emden, *Biographical Register of the University of Oxford*, 3 vols. Oxford 1957–9
CAS	Cambridge Antiquarian Society
C&YS	Canterbury and York Society
CCC	Corpus Christi College, Cambridge
DDC	R. Naz, *Dictionnaire du droit canonique*, 7 vols., Paris 1935–65
Documents	*Documents relating to the university and colleges of Cambridge*, 3 vols., London 1852
EDR	Ely diocesan records, in ULC
EHR	*English Historical Review*
G&C	Gonville and Caius College, Cambridge
JEH	*Journal of Ecclesiastical History*
LAO	Lincolnshire Archives Office
PCAS	*Proceedings of the Cambridge Antiquarian Society*
PRO	Public Record Office
QCC	Queens' College, Cambridge
QCO	The Queen's College, Oxford
SS	Surtees Society
TCBS	*Transactions of the Cambridge Bibliographical Society*
TRHS	*Transactions of the Royal Historical Society*
UA	Cambridge University Archives, in ULC; see D.M. Owen, *Cambridge University Archives: a Classified List*, Cambridge 1988
ULC	University Library, Cambridge
VCH	*Victoria History of the Counties of England*

I

The teaching and study of the canon law
in the later middle ages

IF THIS WERE a sermon and I were permitted a bidding prayer, whose gifts and whose work could I more properly ask you to remember than those of Christopher Cheney, whom, in the words of an anonymous Cambridge canonist, I am proud to hail as *reverende mee domine et magister*?[1] Without the encouragement he began to give me more than forty years ago I should never have launched on this study. I can only hope that he will approve.

I propose to discuss the teaching and practice of the canon law in medieval England and especially, but not exclusively, in Cambridge and eastern England. Today I shall look at our own faculty of canon law in Cambridge, the provision made in the university and colleges for teaching in it, and the accumulation in public and private libraries of appropriate texts for the instruction of its students. Having thus considered provision for training, I propose to devote my next hour to the opportunities for employment to which a canonist might look and to examine such records as survive of their activities in employment. I shall devote my third hour to a more detailed examination of compilations made by canonists themselves, which have survived in some quantity. The faculty of canon law was terminated by the royal injunctions of 1535,[2] but ten years later, pending a reform of the church law which never in fact materialised, members of the faculty of civil law inherited the functions, and many of the subjects of study of the canonists, by an act of Parliament which empowered them to exercise ecclesiastical jurisdiction.[3] It is at this inheritance, and its bibliographical implications, which I propose to look in the final lecture.

Archbishop Winchelsey's official remarked to Simon of Gandavo, bishop of Salisbury, early in the fourteenth century, that clerks so ignorant of the canon law that they made mistakes even in straight-forward appeals to the court of Canterbury, should not be tolerated in a diocesan secretariate.[4] Criticisms of this sort exemplified a new professionalism in diocesan administration and for this the universities were, increasingly, called on to provide vocational training. The result, for the universities, was in fact, a boom in the faculty of canon law (one can provide, in Gilbertian phrase, a little list of contemporary parallels), which ended only in 1535. What this vocational training embraced, after a preliminary study of the Roman, or civil law, was a detailed textual study of the canon law, as it was set forth in the classic texts of the *Decretum* (which consisted of patristic texts, conciliar decrees, and papal decisions, put together and codified about 1140, by Gratian, as *Concordantia discordantium canonum*), together with further papal decisions embodied in the *Decretals*, authorised by Pope Gregory IX in 1234, the *Sext*, or sixth book of decretals, issued by Pope Boniface VIII in 1298, and the *Clementines* of Pope Clement V which appeared in 1317. Soon after, Pope John XXII issued a further series of decretals known as *Extravagantes*, and finally, in the late fifteenth century, a further collection, *Extravagantes Communes*, was authorised.[5]

Meanwhile, from the early thirteenth century, English bishops and archbishops had promulgated in their synods and provincial councils a series of statutes which repeated and amplified papal legislation in the light of specific English needs. Moreover two papal legates, Otto and Ottobuono, had during the reign of Henry III issued statutes for the English church, and these legatine statutes were commented on and glossed by a Cambridge graduate, John of Athon, or Acton. Another famous Cambridge canonist, William Lyndwode, official of Canterbury in Archbishop Chichele's time, and later bishop of St David's, codified English synodal legislation in an imposing work called *Provinciale seu Constituciones Anglie*, which he completed in the years 1422 to 1430. The works of Lyndwode and Acton formed no part of the formal teaching at Cambridge, but, as we shall see, both were studied, and widely applied, by the students of the law faculty.[6]

The sort of detailed knowledge which was acquired by the canonist from his lectures and studies in 'the doctrine of canon and civil law by which the universal church is governed',[7] was demanded by every sort of ecclesiastical business in the later middle ages. A clerk could not resign a benefice, appoint an official deputy, or conduct an election, a layman could not begin or continue a cause in an ecclesiastical court, or bring a will to probate if he did not employ a legally qualified proctor to draw up and present the appropriate documents. A bishop's or archdeacon's affairs could only be carried on with legal advice from men skilled in the law (*iuris periti*). A royal government needed to be represented in diplomatic business by men skilled in the Roman (civil) law, and many of our canonists were, in fact, royal clerks so employed.

Fig. 1 Initial of a charter of King Edward I to the University of
Cambridge showing the king with four doctors, two of canon
law and two of civil law, 1291/2 (UA Luard 7★)

Even at a humbler level much international commerce, and the civic
negotiations it might involve, and many public statements for which
an authentication was required, called for the services of a notary
public.[8] Such men, licensed by papal or imperial authority to draw up
and validate agreements and compositions of all sorts, in the tradition
of the Roman law, were in fact very frequently canonists at the outset
of their career. They might even opt to concentrate on notarial work
in a church court, or a diocesan registry. Because of these possibilities
for employment, the study of canon law seemed to many young and
able clerks to offer the sort of multiple choice which we are told
nowadays to expect of accountancy, or law, or computer science; there
was, in consequence something of a scramble to acquire the appropriate qualifications.

It can never have been an easy study to adopt, and the aspirant
canonist must often have found it difficult to launch out on it, and even
harder to find funds enough to stay the course. The faculty of canon
law had certainly been in existence in Cambridge, with a bedell of its
own, since 1276, and perhaps from 1245.[9] Those entering it were
already masters in the faculty of arts, either in Cambridge or elsewhere.

3

The evolution of the statutes which regulated their courses is almost as difficult to trace as Professor Boyle found it for Oxford,[10] but when the scheme was fully developed the requirements seem to be as follows.[11] A bachelor in the faculty, if he had already ruled in arts, was to hear lectures on civil law and the decretals, for three years each, and then to spend two years hearing the decretum. After this he became an inceptor, and was required to have spent five years on the civil law, three years on the decretals, and two years on the Bible and on the tracts on simony, matrimony, penitence, and consecration, that is, cc. 27 to 36 of part 2 of the decretum. In this period of study he was to read cursory (afternoon) lectures on one of the tracts, and all books of the decretals except the fourth (*de sponsalibus et matrimonio*), and to oppose, when called on, in disputations in the schools. Those who aspired to the doctoral chair were required to spend four further years on civil law and the decretals, unless they had already completed these courses, and were required to borrow, or buy, for their own use, copies of the *corpus iuris civilis* and of the decretum and decretals. The canonist regent masters read the ordinary (morning) lectures, with deputies acting as extraordinary additional lecturers; the business of these ordinary lecturers was to distinguish and comment on the main points to be studied, in their own words, while the bachelors of the faculty were to read cursorily during the afternoons, 'going over' the words of the texts and the glosses. There is an amusing memorandum, in a manuscript of Cambridge provenance now in Oxford, advising the cursory lecturer to follow the precepts of the canonist Hostiensis in his summa, *Titulus de magistris* 'first putting the case, or declaring the sense of the letter, secondly reading the letter, and construing if it seems difficult, thirdly adducing parallels, fourthly noting contrary points, fifthly mentioning noteworthy cases to which the decretal can be applied. But there are some men who merely read the gloss, as if it were the text, which pleases only idiots.'[12]

The substance of canon law teaching has left few manuscripts in Cambridge and even the Oxford law school has yielded relatively few examples. For Cambridge we have what seems to be the formal transcript of a disputation about rights of presentation, which has been copied into the fly leaves of a Gonville and Caius manuscript which has usually been associated with Walter of Elvedon.[13] Among the manuscript fragments used as covers for some of the court books of the Chancellor's court is one which seems to contain notes on the tractate on penitence, *Summula Commedi de penitentia*, while another has portions of what seems to be a *consultatio* (a brief, as it were), about a disputed papal provision.[14] As yet we have found no examples of lecture notes such as Professor Boyle records for fourteenth-century Oxford. On the other hand the Oxford manuscript just quoted contains a series of notes, memoranda, and texts written by one about to occupy the doctor's chair in the school of canon law.[15]

He cites a series of formal prefaces to be spoken by the doctor before he proceeds to his discourse, during the Vespers, or the ceremony of creation:

Having called on the name of Christ, and implored the help of the Blessed Virgin with your [his auditors'] support I turn to the rubric *Iusticia, Capitulum de excepcionibus* . . .

Lest I seem to be speaking too presumptuously before so many skilled in the law and in other sciences I should never proceed to read what I have to say without the correction and improvement of my reverend lord and master R.N. doctor of decrees, who adorns this occasion with his bodily presence; I submit myself also to the correction of my special master Mr. William N., who is the ordinary lecturer in this holy law, and to the comments and corrections of all other doctors, inceptors, bachelors and scholars here present . . .

It must often have been difficult for would-be canonists to support themselves throughout so heroic a course, and there are many indications of the straits to which they were driven. We shall see later how often they relied on the patronage of relatives and friends to acquire the necessary books, or laboriously made their own copies of the indispensable texts. Yet for day-to-day living they very often sought a benefice and a dispensation to absent themselves from it, in conformity with the papal constitution *Cum ex eo*.[16] There were many would-be canonists among the Cambridge scholars who petitioned the Holy See for provision to benefices during the later fourteenth century,[17] and all episcopal registers of the period record the institution of large numbers of such men. Some, even when beneficed, found it necessary to pick up a living, and experience, either in the courts of their own diocese (*in patria*) or in an ecclesiastical court readily available in Cambridge or the neighbourhood. Here the consistory and archdeaconry of Ely, the Chancellor's court, the archdeaconry of Huntingdon and the monastic liberty of Bury St Edmund's absorbed numbers of such men. Wherever this practical experience was acquired it might well be regarded as a qualification towards graduation: the first Grace Books record many such examples as this of 1460: 'Mr. David Blodwell and Mr. Hugh Tapton, having studied five years in canon law (two years in *lectura* in a hall for scholars, two years in hearing the decretum, and one year the Bible), together with seven years in practice in the courts, are allowed to incept in both laws.'[18] The parallel with a modern sandwich course is hard to avoid.

Other canonists went much further afield, usually in attendance on patrons, and it must often have seemed like exile to do so, as is suggested by a letter copied into the Oxford manuscript from a Cambridge scholar exiled in Colchester, to a friend lucky enough to remain in paradise in Cambridge. He writes in the silence of the night and tries in vain to console himself with *pestifero morbo vini*. He and other Cambridge friends remember the attempt of the university authorities to interfere with such laudable customs as the doffing of caps and biretta during vespers and other disputations. These were the men to whom the faculty of canon law was a splendid home, which one of them celebrated in an invocation which Professor Logan has published from this same manuscript:

> O facultas canonica
> Que splendes sicut sidera
> Qui te honorant proinde
> Ditasti multo munere
> Gloria tibi domina
> Per quam ornatur ecclesia . . .[19]

The teaching offered by the faculty of canon law had certainly been provided long before 1300, in a house of scholars owned by one Nicholas de Barber, a Cambridge burgess, opposite Great St Mary, where canonists, legists, and occasionally theologians, were used to lecture.[20] This house was surrendered to Nicholas in 1309, and there is no clear indication where legal teaching was done until, about 1440, a school of canon law was equipped in the common schools (the old schools), below the new library.[21] But before this time several hostels, at first privately owned, seem to have taken the place of the lost house, and become, not so much centres of legal studies, as places to which would-be canonists and legists would resort. At least eight of these hostels were marked as *hospitia iuristariorum* in Richard Lyne's 1574 map of Cambridge and there are many casual references which show that jurists seeking employment or dispensation lived in such places. St Clement's hostel, on the south corner of St Clement's churchyard, housed ecclesiastical lawyers until 1640, but the best known of all was Burdon Hostel or Inn, which lay between Green Street and Rose Crescent, and the ownership of which was shared between Peterhouse

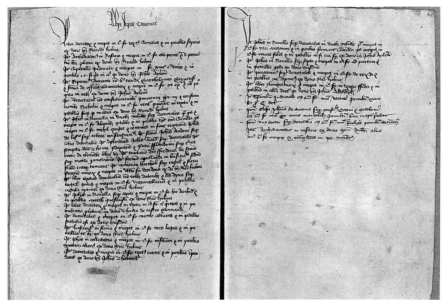

Fig. 2   List of canon law texts belonging to the university of
Cambridge in 1424 (UA Coll. Admin. 4, f. 44v)

and Clare Hall. Here the principals were almost all canonists, active not
only in the faculty, but also in the Ely courts, and here, it is clear, much
formal teaching, and a good deal of unofficial study, went on.[22]

The provision of books for this highly popular and expensive study
began only slowly. There seems to have been no serious attempt by the
university to equip a library for lawyers until about 1424, when a list of
books belonging to the university includes twenty-seven works classed
as *libri iuris canonici*.[23] Of these, eight were canonical texts and the rest
fairly commonplace commentaries, glosses, and *repertoria*: Archdeacon Guy de Basio (*in Rosario*) on the Sext, John Andreas (the
Novella) on decretals and Sext, Bartholomew of Brescia (Brixiensis) on
the decretum, a collection of cases of conscience drawn from the
decretals, Dynus (Magellanus) on the rules of law, Durandus' *Repertorium* and *Speculum Iudiciale*, Hostiensis' *Summa Copiosa* and *Lectura*,
Pope Innocent IV on the decretals. Some of these had been bequests:
Mr Richard de Holme, for instance, bequeathed to the university a
decretum, an Archdeacon, decretals, Hostiensis, and Innocent which
he had himself inherited from Richard Ravenser archdeacon of
Lincoln, who had died in 1385.[24] Before the disappearance of the
faculty the university's collection had been much augmented by

7

further bequests, as Henry Bradshaw's paper on the library has shown.[25] Yet it remains true that most of the Cambridge bequests, even before the late fourteenth century, were already going to the relatively new institutions, the colleges, and it is to these that we must now turn.

It was in the colleges that student places were endowed, and specialised library provision made. The medieval colleges were from the first thought of as post-graduate establishments, providing not for grammarians, or artists, but for students in the higher faculties of theology, medicine, and law. So large was the demand for lawyers that observers of the Cambridge scene must from the beginning have feared that such men would, unless restricted, absorb all the resources of the new institutions. This seems to explain the complete exclusion of lawyers in the foundation statutes of some colleges, and the rigid restriction of numbers in others. At Peterhouse the original statutes, usually dated to 1284, stipulate only that no more than two fellows should be legists, and that one should study medicine, and this provision was repeated in the revision of 1344. It is perhaps worth remarking that among those who worked hardest for the college was the bishop's chancellor, Robert Worth, a very distinguished canonist. Clare Hall preferred its fellows to be theologians, apart from one legist and one student of medicine. Pembroke Hall imposed no quota, while King's Hall, intended by Edward II and his son to be a nursery of royal servants, was occupied by civilians and a small number of canonists. It was here that a lectureship in canon law, to be open to the whole university, was endowed by John Bellamy in 1494.[26]

With Gonville Hall and Trinity Hall we come to more precise provision for legal studies, and this is not surprising when we remember that each was essentially the creation of the distinguished canonist William Bateman, bishop of Norwich. In Gonville there appears to be no limit placed on the numbers of legists in the college and a weekly provision was stipulated of disputations in theology, philosophy, civil, and canon law within the college: it seems likely, as Professor Brooke has recently remarked, that in this provision Walter Elvedon, who had been Bateman's chancellor, and was one of the original fellows, may have been particularly strong.[27] For Trinity Hall the provision was more explicit: it was to be

ad cultus divini ac scientie canonice et civilis ... unum perpetuum collegium scolarium iuris canonici et civilis in universitate Cantabrigiensi.

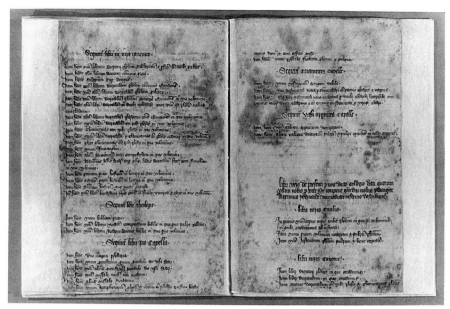

Fig. 3 List of canon law texts given to Trinity Hall by its founder Bishop William Bateman before his death (UA Luard 39)

There were to be between ten and thirteen civilians and seven and ten canonists, three weekly disputations in canon and civil law were to be attended by all members of the college, and a special endowment of appropriate books was made, thirty of civil law and thirty-five of canon law: these were not to leave the college, except for use in the schools.[28] The statutes of Corpus Christi required all fellows to proceed to the study of theology. King's on the other hand placed no restrictions on the study of its fellows, and even provided for the payment of lecturers in theology, civil, and canon law who were to work within the college. The college *mundum* books record payments for canon law lectures made to members of the college, Mr Geoffrey and Mr Combe, in the years 1468–9 and 1469–70.[29] By contrast Queens' refused to allow a fellow to study law until he had ruled in arts for three years, while St Catharine's, by its statutes, permitted no explicitly legist fellows.[30]

So much for the actual provision of places and maintenance for lawyers, but how else were their studies fostered? The need for multiple copies of standard texts and the protection of the book stock from loss and theft is clearly demonstrated in the arrangements for the Peterhouse library. There were before 1300 a series of books chained in the library, and others which were available for distribution. The chained books were the standard texts, the decretum, decretals, and so on, together with such standard commentaries as John Andreas, the Archdeacon, Innocent IV, and Hostiensis. Bequests later added to the stock Sampson on the Extravagants, Lyndwode's *Provinciale*, and the legatine constitutions. Second copies of these and similar works were made available for distribution, along with Bernard of Parma's *Casus super decretales*.[31] Bishop Bateman's foundation gift to Trinity Hall included one decretum, eight decretals, most glossed, four Sexts and Clementines, with William de Monte Laudino's gloss on the Clementines, and the treatises of John Andreas on the decretals and the rules of law, as well as Hostiensis' *Summa copiosa* and *lectura*. He proposed to bequeath after his death further copies of the decretum, decretals, Sext, and Clementines (two of these), William de Monte Laudino, John Andreas, and Hostiensis. More unusually, he proposed to leave the college 'a compilation of allegations and decisions of doubtful points in the Roman curia' (a precursor perhaps of Fastolf). There were other bequests to Trinity Hall of the Sext, Clementines, Innocent IV, and John Andreas, by Adam de Wickmer, examiner general of the court of Canterbury, all to be chained.[32]

The Old Master's Book of Clare Hall records many gifts to the college of canon law texts, during the fourteenth century: Thomas Asteley gave one copy of the decretals; Mr John de Donewich after 1371 contributed a summa of Hostiensis, the Archdeacon, and John Andreas' *Novella*. Dr Thomas Lexham, who had been Bateman's chamberlain, and died in 1382, made an unusual bequest, of works perhaps acquired during his residence in Avignon: by Persivall, John Faventinus, Ruffinus, and Stephen of Besançon. When a library list was compiled in the fifteenth century it included under *Ius canonicum*, in addition to the standard texts and the commentaries bequeathed by Lexham and Donewich, Reimundus, Innocent IV, and Lyndwode's *Provinciale*.[33]

Despite its restriction of its fellows to the study of theology Pembroke Hall had received from William Styburd, some time after 1351, a decretum, decretals, Sext (now Pembroke ms. 165), a summa and apparatus on Innocent IV (Pembroke ms. 188), the constitutions of Lambeth and a commentary on the Sext called *Rosarium*.[34] Corpus too received a few conventional texts to be allotted to the fellows, from

Thomas Markaunt: the decreta with a *casuarium* on it, a *tabula martiana*, and a copy of the *pupilla oculi* (a summary of the canon law for the use of the parochial clergy).[35] By 1391 King's Hall too had a small supply of conventional texts. A decretum, Archdeacon, Innocent IV, two copies of the Sext, and Durandus' *Speculum* were chained; in addition there were two copies of the decretals, Sext, John Andreas', Dinus' rules of law in two copies, and the glosses of Vincent on the decretals and William de Monte Lauduno on the Clementines. Some of these had been acquired by bequests and the college in 1416 received other gifts from William de Waltham, further copies of John Andreas, Dinus, and Durandus as well as John de Limano on the Clementines.[36]

Perhaps the most important bequests made to a college, apart from the founder's benefaction at Trinity Hall, are those received by Gonville Hall from Walter of Elvedon (Bateman's vicar general) who bequeathed Durandus, with his own *tabula copiosissima* (ms. 254), John Andreas (ms. 483), and a collection of civil law tracts with a canonistic *questio disputata* entered on the flyleaves. Thomas Cabold about 1500 added the commentaries of John Andreas and others on the Sext, Godfrey of Trano on the decretals, and the summa of Reymund of Pennaforte (mss. 45, 172, 380).[37]

Towards the end of the medieval period such non-canonist colleges as Queens' had also acquired a few basic canonist texts. In 1478, for example, Robert Bryan, DCnL, bequeathed to it Peter of Anchorano on the decretals, Zabarella *De casibus iuris*, the *Decisiones nove* of the *auditorum rote* and the decretals with the gloss of John the monk. Queens' too received Zabarella, in a printed edition (QCC 11.4) from William Rede, and John Andreas and Acton's gloss on the legatine constitutions came before 1484 from Thomas Welles, advocate of the consistory of Norwich.[38]

At least one hostel received a canonist's library: in 1529 Burdon's Inn was allotted a number of texts from the estate of John Dowman, who in 1526 had bequeathed to the university all his 'chief books of councils and doctors, of the law', duplicates to be put into Clement Hostel. A receipt from the principal of Burdon's Inn is entered in the Junior Proctor's book and shows it to be almost entirely printed editions of conciliar decrees and commentaries of John of Imola, Zabarella, John Andreas, Baldus, Bowycius, and Abbas (figure 4).[39]

Many of these bequests give clues to the types of private library owned by individual canonists teaching within the university, or practising in the courts, before reaching high office in the church.

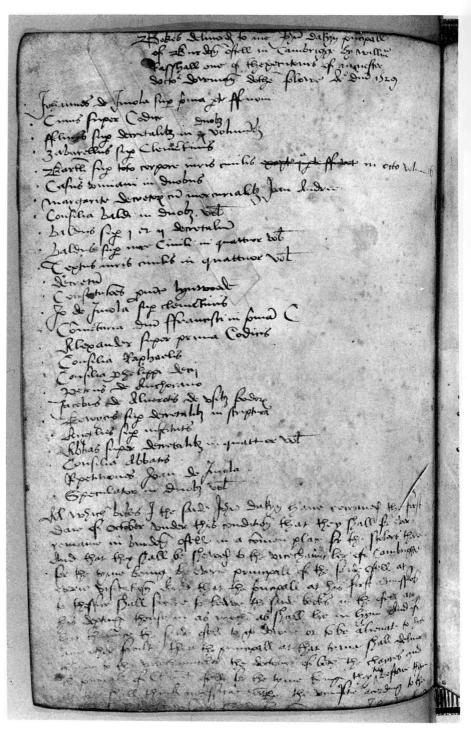

Fig. 4   Legal texts bequeathed to the university by John Dowman and transmitted by his executors to the lawyers' hostel, Burdon Hostel, 1529 (UA Coll. Admin. 2, f. 153v)

Henry Bowet, archbishop of York, who died in 1423, had a large library, the inventory of which has survived and included:

liber vocatus Gratianus super certis articulis decretorum
liber vocatus distinciones fratris Johannis Bromyerd super certos titulos iuris civilis et
    canonici
liber decretorum
liber vocatus Archidiaconus in Rosario
liber decretalium sed male scribitur
liber sextus cum quatuor doctoribus
liber vocatus Godfridus super titulos decretalium
liber vocatus Johannes in Novella super decretales
liber vocatus Abbas in lectura super titulos decretalium
liber vocatus Hostiensis in lectura
liber vocatus Roffrid' cum aliis tractatibus
liber vocatus Andrewe vetus et debile

Dr John Newton, official of Ely in the early fifteenth century and later official of York, bequeathed his books to York Minster in trust for the studies of his nephews. They included all the usual canon law texts, decretum, decretals, Sext and Clementines, as well as the standard commentaries of Innocent IV, the Archdeacon, Hostiensis, and Durandus.[40]

Individual canonists who deposited their own books with the proctors as pledges (cautions) for the completion of obligatory courses or the payment of rents for the schools, owned a variety of the standard texts: decretum, decretals, Provinciale, and the commentaries of Bernard of Parma, Andrew Vallensis, Archdeacon, John Andreas, John of Ancona, James of Ravenna, Innocent IV, Durandus, and Hostiensis.[41] Other canonists are known to have bequeathed to others, or to have received as bequests, texts the ownership of which can be traced for some distance. Gervase Scrope, canon of Lincoln, bequeathed in 1383 to Richard Scrope, official of Ely, chancellor of the university, auditor of causes of the sacred palace and later archbishop of York, a copy of Hostiensis *in lectura* which passed, with the texts and several glosses of the Sext and Clementines, to Stephen Scrope archdeacon of Richmond, who eventually bequeathed them to William Alnwick, bishop first of Norwich and then of Lincoln.[42]

Other clerical wills show what texts were owned by practising administrators and lawyers. Walter Skirlawe bishop of Durham, for example, owned at his death in 1406 two pairs of decretals, *lectura* on the Clementines by John de Ligno, two commentaries on the decretum by William de Monte Lauduno, and three volumes of John Andreas.

Robert Alne, examiner general of the courts of York bequeathed to the university library in Cambridge works by the Archdeacon, Innocent IV, a paper book of the extravagants, the conclusions of the Rote, and Gosselyn. Charles Bothe, bishop of Lichfield and later of Hereford, bequeathed at his death in 1535 to Hereford cathedral a number of printed texts including the decretum, *extravagantes communes*, Lyndwode, Zabarella, Anchorano, Koelner de Vankel, and Bartholomew of Brescia. Even so late as 1546 William Davy of King's Hall owned at his death decretum, decretals, Sext, and Clementines, two copies of Bernard of Parma, and Dynus' rules of law.[43]

None of these professional libraries (we do not of course usually know their complete extent) comes near to the great collection of William Doune archdeacon of Leicester, a very distinguished canonist whose will was admirably analysed by Professor Hamilton Thompson, and whose books were distributed to a large number of beneficiaries drawn from his official staff and his immediate family, and to the abbey of Osney.[44] The books of Walter Stapeldon bishop of Exeter and founder of Exeter College also make an impressive show in the inventory drawn up at his death in 1328; many had been inherited from John Mounghithe. They invariably included multiple copies of the canonical texts and glosses, apparatus and lectures of Archdeacon, Huguccio, Peter de Salnis, Hostiensis, Innocent IV, Bartholomew of Brescia, and John Andreas.[45] Walter de Trefnant bishop of Bath and Wells about 1401 owned twenty-six canonical texts of some importance, mostly, it seems, intended for teaching; to this list we shall return in the third lecture.[46] Finally the large library of Martin Colyns, canon of York, who died in 1509, included many printed copies of modern European works.[47]

Individual scholars must often have found it hard, at the outset of their course, to provide themselves with the necessary texts if they had no access to copies in school or college libraries. Many relied on loans from older relatives or connections (Dr Emden's *Biographical Registers* note many of these), or from a monastic or parochial library near their home. In 1511, for example, the schoolmaster of Alford in Lincolnshire, Arthur Waddington, borrowed from the small Premonstratensian house of Hagnaby the *decretum*, digest (of the civil law), *pupilla oculi*, and *casus decreti*, plainly with a view of a grounding in the canon law.[48] Surviving inventories of church furniture made in the fourteenth century, such as those compiled for the archdeacons of Ely and Norwich, show that many parish churches had acquired and retained copies of the synodal statutes and of *pupilla oculi*. Many bishops required parish priests to own and read the statutes, and two examples of such books from the diocese of Ely have recently come to light.[49] There are thus a number of places from which the impoverished scholar could borrow his books.

A number of surviving manuscripts show the devices which were used to simplify the acquisition of the contents of texts and glosses. Peterhouse ms. 42, for example, contains a series of indices and alphabetical tables for the works of the Archdeacon and Bernard of Parma. It also has glossaries, word lists, even mnemonic verses on the contents of the books of the decretals:

> pars prior officia creat ecclesie et ministros
> altera dat testes et creat iudiciorum
> tercia de rebus et vita presbiterorum
> dat normam recte nubere quarta decet
> quintaque de viciis et peius tractat eorum.

Peterhouse ms. 264 is a metrical version of the whole of the decretals, and Corpus Christi ms. 38 is a similar collection of verses on Innocent IV's 'margarita' on the decretum. Others have come to light in a fragmentary state, and re-used fragments in book covers can probably be attributed to similar groups.

Walter of Elvedon made his own tabula (an alphabetical index) on the Sext, which is now Peterhouse ms. 42, and other, humbler, scholars constructed their own apparatus, like the table of provincial constitutions made by or for Mr John Wortham, rector of Fowlmire, which now forms part of Trinity College ms. 1245. The library of Gonville and Caius includes several of these learning aids: ms. 30/19 for example contains Sampson de Calvo Monte's abbreviation of Hostiensis' *in lectura*. Ms. 54/31, a compilation said to have been Elvedon's, contains a *libellum super iure canonico*, a *libellum de excepcionibus et modus procedendi in causa*. Ms. 67/34 is an abbreviated decretum and mss. 262 and 263 are both tables of Lyndwode.

There are in the University Library two manuscripts related to these miscellaneous aids to learning. Ms. Mm.4.41, of apparently unknown provenance, is a varied compilation. It begins with Archbishop Stratford's constitutions and other provincial legislation; the second part has an index to the Sext, *summule* of different parts of the decretum and of Hostiensis' *Summa aurea*, probably intended for beginners, and a copy of a Cambridge statute concerning hostels. The volume is completed by materials about sins and sacraments, perhaps prepared for the use of parish priests and penitentiaries, and drawn partly from the works of John Andreas. Ms. Additional 3467, once Phillips 2278, is a series of abbreviated extracts from the decretals, which the explicit calls *Notabilia decretorum*. It contains a series of short summaries of the decretum and decretals prepared by, or for a lecturer: it may well have been used for cursory teaching at a rather elementary level. Individual words are distinguished by pointing hands with obvious statements: 'NICHIL nota diversitas verborum non obstat ubi eadem sententia reperitur.'

It seems likely that a number of the best Cambridge canonistic manuscripts must have been lost at, or soon after, the demise of the faculty and nowhere, not even in Gonville and Caius, have we a surviving group to match the examples in, for example, New College, Oxford. Here ms. 182 contains Peter of Anchorano's commentary on the Clementines and a copy of the Extravagants, which were a gift from the founder. There are three copies of Henry de Bohic's commentaries and summa of the decretals, and two copies of Innocent IV, one of which is associated with the distinguished canonist Adam of Orleton. Ms. 192 includes the text of a lecture on book I of the decretals composed by R. of Wodestok or Heete, who declares himself to have been (in 1415) the pupil of Mr William Barow, chancellor of the university. MS. 197 appears to have been another teaching aid consisting of a catechism on books III and IV of the decretals. There are examples of the usual commentaries of John Andreas and Bartholomew of Brescia, and so on, and perhaps the most unusual text is an alphabetical analysis of the three laws, divine, canon, and civil, said to have been compiled by John Bromyard OP of Cambridge.[50]

The end of all this came suddenly: for official purposes the injunctions of the royal visitors of 1535 forbade the teaching and examination of the canon law in the university, and this, so far as the fragmentary sources allow us to discover, is what happened. There appear to be no canonist graduates after this date.

II

Canonists and their careers

IN A QUEEN'S College, Oxford, manuscript from which I have already quoted there is copied, apparently for its elegant Latinity, a letter from a Cambridge scholar to a friend with whom he had 'learned from our common mother the University, the health giving sweet savour of the law'. It is written from exile at Colchester in the silence of the night and is full of the sorrow of a man excluded from a Cambridge paradise.[1] It epitomises the dilemma of a scholar who yearned to go on studying the law with his friends, but is obliged to find a place and earn his living. He resolves 'having put his hand to the plough, to continue in the way'. The writer is facing a problem with which we are all familiar. One cannot remain a student of the canon law for ever. What does one do, and for what is one now equipped? To what, in fact does this long and expensive training lead?

One might, and many did, regard it as a preliminary to the public service and diplomacy and this was especially true for doctors of both laws, who were equipped by their studies in civil law to meet and bargain at the courts of western Europe. The extended negotiations of the Hundred Years War and the Conciliar Movement afforded ample scope for the expertise of such men, and opportunities could still be grasped, even on the eve of the Reformation. Thomas Cromwell, while still a humble hanger-on of Wolsey gave legal, financial, and practical advice to the secretary of the gild of the Blessed Virgin in Boston during the campaign to obtain a papal indulgence for the gild. Cromwell and the secretary, Geoffrey Chambers, went together to Calais and Rome twice between 1517 and 1520, and Cromwell was paid over £100 for his services, which were clearly partly legal. I do not know whether Cromwell could properly be called *iuris peritus*, but it is certain that he, and probably many others, knew the uses to which a knowledge of the law could be put.[2]

Other humble canonists and civilians might attach themselves as legal secretaries and engrossers of documents to the households of abbots, priors, and collegiate foundations, especially if they had qualified themselves as notaries public. The earlier years of Thomas

Snappe, whose notebook (if it *is* his) I shall discuss in the next lecture, were passed in such occupations, and in Cambridge, Robert Brydon, BCL, a married clerk from the diocese of York, was from 1461 occupied in and about Cambridge and Ely.[3] He was intermittently employed by Peterhouse and Corpus Christi and in the household of the prior at Ely. Geoffrey Chambers, the secretary of the Boston Gild, seems to have passed on to profitable service in the court of Augmentations.[4] The university, too, afforded some employment for such men: John Brokeshaw of Kings', for example, MA and notary public, wrote official letters not only for Corpus Christi, but also for the university in the seventies and eighties of the fifteenth century.[5] There must always have been a few such men in the neighbourhood of the law schools, but the fourteenth and fifteenth centuries, as collegiate foundations multiplied and the university administration was increasingly professionalised, increased the number of opportunities for employment of a casual and intermittent type.

For permanent employment, however, the canonist and even the civilian must turn to the church itself, which sometimes offered the highest rewards and might lead the very fortunate to a bishopric. There was, it seems, a recognisable career structure, a *cursus honorum* in diocesan administration, as the late Brian Woodcock pointed out when discussing the diocesan courts of Canterbury, and as Professor Storey has elaborated, chiefly for the fifteenth-century courts of Durham.[6] Storey distinguished the permanent hierarchy of officers in the courts from the household of the bishop himself, with its *familia* of legal experts and secretaries, from among whom the court of audience, which remained close to the bishop's person, was staffed.

The courts certainly absorbed a great many clerks, despite the efforts of some bishops and archbishops to restrict the numbers of advocates and proctors practising in them. At Exeter, where Bishop Stapeldon visited the consistory in 1323, there were two examiners, nine advocates or expectants, eight proctors or expectants, a notary, two clerks, and an apparitor, besides the presiding judge or official.[7] This was only one of several courts within the diocese, for the archdeaconries and peculiar jurisdictions had each their own judge and lesser officials. Despite some pluralism in the higher ranges, there is nevertheless a fair number of posts. To these one must add a range of posts in the bishop's household, and in those of the archdeacons, and in the larger dioceses, notably London, Lincoln, and Norwich, those of the episcopal commissaries. For the relatively small diocese of Worcester, Professor

Haines mentions episcopal clerks, who were multi-purpose, vicar general, auditor of causes, official, sequestrator, chancellor, commissary-general, registrar, scribe, notary, apparitor, receiver, and messenger.[8] Similar, though slightly diverging patterns can be detected in the entries of every episcopal register, and most archdeacons had similar but smaller numbers of functionaries. There was, indeed, a veritable army of clerical administrators.

The initial recruitment of the members of this bureaucracy poses a number of problems. There is sometimes an easy answer: a new bishop or archdeacon liked to bring in his own men. Bishop Gainsborough took with him to Worcester in 1303 a number of Lincolnshire men and Bishop Roger Martival of Salisbury, who was a Leicester man who had been dean of Lincoln, had men in his household who must have been with him since his early days.[9] There is nothing peculiar to the middle ages in this; it is a phenomenon which can be observed today, yet the impulse to recruit and retain men from one's own locality was never stronger than in the later medieval centuries and the careers of some very successful administrators can be explained by this sort of locality tie. William Courtenay, the well-born clerk who rose rapidly through the chancellorship of Oxford and the sees of Hereford and London to become archbishop of Canterbury in 1379, had an extended entourage of clerks from his own diocese of Exeter, who may well have been fellow students with him in Stapeldon Hall (Exeter College). These men followed him from Oxford to Hereford and London, and most of them appear as legal assessors at the Blackfriars Council of 1382, in which, in the first great crisis of Courtenay's pontificate, the teachings of Wycliffe were condemned. Some of these men had already moved away from the archbishop's service: some had become diocesan officials, like John Lydford at Winchester, or advocates in the court of Canterbury, like the brothers Baldwin and John Shillingford, or even bishops, as the brothers Robert and Nicholas Braybroke had done. Some would go back in the end to their native diocese: Lydford and Ralph Tregrisiou were cathedral dignitaries in Exeter at their deaths.[10]

The life of William Doune, whose unusually detailed will has survived, seems to be fairly characteristic of the careers of clerical administrators. He began, in his native Exeter, as a notary, and later registrar, in the household of Bishop John Grandisson; he was beneficed there, received a dispensation for study of the canon law, and from that point on moved into other diocesan service until he became archdeacon of Leicester. In his turn Doune arranged for the legal education of his two nephews and of a clerk and notary who were in his archidiaconal household.[11]

The large number of clerical bequests to clerk-protégés for the furtherance of their education suggests that the aspirants were often poor, and humble in origin, although this can scarcely be proved conclusively. John Lydford bequeathed ten pounds to his clerk James Carslegh, who subsequently held various offices in the Exeter courts and household, and who, as we shall see, inherited and amplified Lydford's professional notebook.

It was in the Exeter pontificate of Walter Stapeldon, 1308 to 1326, and during the long period of William Bateman's curial service, which ended with his death in 1355, that the full tide of lawyer administrators reached the English church. Stapeldon, who had himself taught canon law in Oxford, had in his own household at least one lawyer, Robert Herward, his own connection and a future archdeacon of Taunton. Nevertheless his principal contribution to the church was undoubtedly the college he founded, which was soon dominated by canonists.[12] Bateman, *utriusque iuris peritorum flos precipuus*, by his central position as royal proctor and auditor of the palace in Avignon, was an immensely important patron and source of inspiration to English canonists on the way up. Members of his household were among the leading ecclesiastical figures of the century: Henry de Chaddesden, Robert Herward, John de Ufford, and the future archbishop Simon Sudbury, had all been his protégés and at the time of his death in 1355 his household in Avignon included seven canonists.[13] A whole generation after Bateman's death, Lydford copied two of his opinions, perhaps acquired from Herward, into his notebook, and a particularly good example of his influence can be seen in the first chapter act book at Salisbury, where the diocesan official Thomas de Astley records a consultation in a difficult patronage case:[14] 'I sent the whole account of the matter, together with certain legal arguments advanced by both sides, to my Lord Bishop of Norwich who is most skilled and knowledgeable about such matters.' He received in return a reasoned exposition of the case, which is copied into the act book. Nothing demonstrates more clearly the important position accorded at this time to legal expertise.

The episcopal household was in general headed by the official principal although he might well share his responsibilities with others, especially in the larger dioceses. Such a man would often be at the summit of his profession, frequently a doctor of both laws. He would preside in the principal court of the diocese (the consistory), he would lead the council of several *iuris periti* who advised the bishop. At all times he was the *organum vocis* of the bishop, preparing and reading his arbitrations and judgments. At times the official of Ely was a canonist of some distinction; several had served as chancellor of the university and went on to the higher reaches of clerical office, usually via the court of Canterbury, and often also in the papal chancery. Perhaps the most notable was Richard Scrope, chancellor of the university, papal chaplain, and eventually archbishop of York, who met his end in 1405 as leader of a northern rebellion against Henry IV.[15]

The record of the official's activity can best be seen in the register of the consistory. This has sometimes come to be bound as part of the episcopal register, and there is a good example for Rochester where the latter part of Hamo de Hethe's register is devoted to *acta iudicialia* for the years 1347 and 1348.[16] We are fortunate to have in Ely the first complete register of the consistory, which covers the years 1378 to 1381, and to this I shall return later. The principal assistant of the official was undoubtedly the registrar or scribe of the acts, a notary public and often a canonist, sometimes, like William Doune, starting out in this post for a career which would lead him to much higher things. The registrar was not only responsible for the form of record in the consistory register and that of the bishop, but was also often a remembrancer; the same is true later of the best of our university registraries. Memoranda books compiled by registrars have sometimes survived with the diocesan records to which they relate, but have more often strayed. We have in the University Library's collections two examples of this sort: one Dd. 10.28 from Lincoln, the *Vetus Repertorium* of John de Schalby, the other (Add. 3468), the Black Book of the Consistory of Ely. Comparable collections for the archdeaconry of Ely are preserved in Gonville and Caius, and there is a similar compilation for the archdeaconry of Norwich among the King's Remembrancer's records in the Public Record Office.[17]

One of the chief duties of the episcopal council, which usually included one leading canonist who is sometimes described as the bishop's chancellor, was to hear and determine causes submitted to the bishop's own hearing, his audience. The canon law had said:

Since the bishop is known to have ordinary jurisdiction in his whole diocese there is no doubt that he may freely sit in judgment either in person or through another, to hear causes belonging to the ecclesiastical court in every place that is not exempt from that jurisdiction.[18]

Usually the bishops seem to have reserved for personal hearing matrimonial causes which involved perjury, wilful murder by clerks, usury, breaches of sanctuary, attacks on the property of the church, clerical lapses into sin after a first correction, important probates, and, necessarily, prosecutions of heretics. The record of these audience causes was almost always entered in the episcopal register, except for the largest dioceses, which, towards the end of the middle ages, had begun to set aside a special register of audience business.

Membership of a bishop's council was undoubtedly reserved for those known in some circles as 'high flyers', and their numbers were necessarily small. There were far more opportunities for employment in the diocesan courts, the consistory, commissary courts within the archdeaconries of such larger dioceses as London, Lincoln and Norwich, the archidiaconal courts, the liberties of collegiate churches such as Ripon, Southwell, and Beverley, and almost all secular cathedral chapters. In addition, there were courts in many larger monastic liberties, such as St Alban's, Bury, and Westminster. Cambridge canonists were employed in a wide area of eastern England, certainly from York southwards as far as London. Many began with employment in the Ely courts or those of the university, or in the commissary courts of Huntingdon and Colchester, and the monastic archdeaconry of Sudbury (Bury), where they could practise almost without leaving Cambridge.

The tradition established by Richard Scrope seems to have taken many Cambridge men to York as proctors, advocates, and judges in various courts: the most notable of these was perhaps Dr John Newton, about whose library I spoke in the first lecture. No doubt home connections, and the influence of a patron, determined where the canonist first launched himself. The neighbourhood of a commissary court, and even more of the episcopal commissary himself, was very attractive and I have already referred to what Professor Brundage has described as 'the bar' of the consistory court.[19] Notaries would always be needed in such areas and no doubt a large number gathered, and made themselves useful in the neighbourhood of the court. The numbers of the proctors who represented their clients in court, and advocates, who advised on, and prepared, their causes, were, as we have seen, rigidly restricted in many consistories before the middle of the fourteenth century.

A successful proctor might hope for an advocate's place in the same consistory, or might aspire to higher things as a pleader, or even an official in the courts of Canterbury – Arches, Audience, or Prerogative – until opportunities could be made for recommending oneself to the higher reaches of the establishment. John Lydford, the official of Winchester, of whose book I have spoken, was admitted advocate in the court of Arches early in his career, Thomas of Wormenhale had a spell as auditor in the same court before becoming official of Ely in 1373. William Spalding was examiner-general of the court of Canterbury and Dean of Arches. Still more propitiously the young canonist might leave for the papal curia as the retained, semi-resident proctor of a bishop, a monastery, or a cathedral chapter. Lydford represented archbishops Courtenay and Whittlesey in this way. Alternatively he might make shorter visits to Avignon, and later to Rome, as a representative of individual petitioners. Here William Swan, whose letter-books have been vividly described by E.F. Jacob, is perhaps the leading exponent.[20] A few Englishmen, and notably John Fastolf, whose career in the Rota Professor Baker has recently discussed, themselves became curial officers. Walter Stapeldon, William Bateman, and Simon Sudbury are among the most notable of these. Many who aimed at curial service, especially during and after the end of the Conciliar Movement, sought their training in Bologna, like Archbishop Chichele's nephew William, who sought papal favour while still a student there 'because he intended to engage in the service of the Pope and the Roman Church'.[21]

The papal curia apart, and I do not intend to deal further with its English personnel, the largest English employers of canonists at all times were the courts of Canterbury and York, the episcopal consistories, and the archdeaconry courts. Here, once officially admitted to the bar as a proctor, a man might properly charge fees for services. Local customs about the fees to be charged, and about the number of admitted proctors, varied considerably and it became necessary during the fourteenth century to reduce the customs of many courts to written statutes. There are not many surviving sets of such statutes, but enough have survived to make the general situation clear. At Lincoln, where statutes were promulgated in 1330, no man could become a proctor without four years of study and one year's probation, or advocate unless he had six years' study and a year's experience in fighting causes. In 1391 Bishop Buckingham rebuked the proctors for chattering, and disturbing behaviour, walking to and fro between their seats and the registry, uttering silly and superstitious statements in their clients' defence, caring only about their fees, and treating the court as if it were a tavern. They were ordered to keep their seats while the court was sitting, and to be silent while other proctors addressed the court.[22] The Exeter visitation makes it clear that for every proctor and advocate in place, twice as many were awaiting admission, and were maintaining themselves as notaries, examiners, and even registrars, while they waited. We have not found any Ely statutes but we do at least have record of the oaths required in that court when proctors were admitted: they were chiefly concerned with the proctors' integrity in their handling of causes, especially for miserable and poor clients, for whom examination fees were to be waived.

Few formal records of court proceedings have survived and it is often necessary to look for information about them outside the surviving diocesan records. By the time of which I am talking the conduct of business in the courts was rigidly determined by the provisions of canon law as set out in the second book of decretals: the earnest student would certainly familiarise himself with the requirements of this book and no doubt the *Carmen* reciting the heads of chapters which appears in some printed editions of the *Corpus* was one of the ways of achieving this:

> Iudicium, forus, atque libellus mutua poscens
> Litem contestans sine quo non suscipe testes
> Iurat, dilatis et feriat ordine noscit.[23]

The procedures of the courts were those drawn from the Roman law, which had become usual throughout the western church long before the time with which we are concerned, wherever lawyers trained in the civil and canon law were employed.[24] Causes opened with a request from the plaintiff (*pars actrix*) to the registrar of the court for the citation of the defendant (*pars rea*) to answer a charge. The citation was served by an apparitor, its service was certified to the court, and each side appointed proctors who were admitted to plead by the court. The libel containing the plaintiff's case was then produced and read in court, after which, if the action was plenary, the defendant could make procedural or material exceptions to it, on the value of which the judge must decide before the case could continue. If the exceptions were refused, the court moved forward to the *litis contestacio*, in which the plaintiff's case was again propounded and the defendant denied its points *seriatim*. This denial or *contradiccio* could be a lengthy business, and so might the next stage, when oaths *de calumnia*

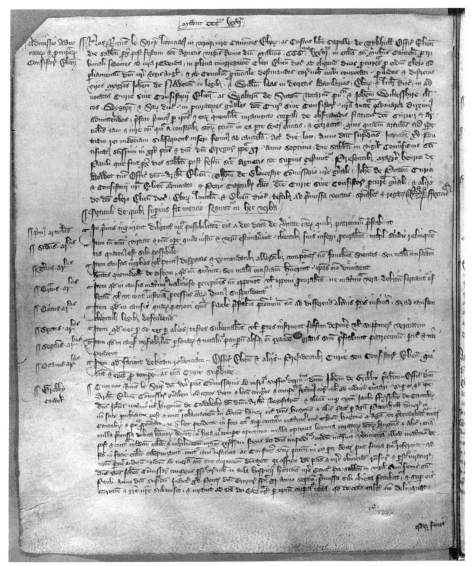

Fig. 5 Procedures to be followed by proctors in the court of
Ely 1375 (EDR D2/1, f. 62v)

and *de veritate dicenda* were taken by both parties: it was open to each
side to refuse these oaths. Once they were taken the plaintiff proceeded
to prove his case. The articles of his libel were once more read over, the
defendant, replying through his proctor, as at all points in the case,
answered 'yes' or 'no' to each; witnesses were named, cited, sworn, and
deposed to the truth or falsity of each point. The depositions they made

were taken down in writing by examiners and copies supplied to the defendant, who might then except in writing to the character of the witnesses, or the bias of the evidence; these exceptions would then be proved by depositions from a fresh set of witnesses. Finally, when the plaintiff was satisfied that his case was established, he moved for a 'term to propound all acts' and this was followed by a petition for sentence. The sentence repeated the substance of this libel, and accepted or rejected the plaintiff's proofs and a final term was assigned for the taxation or assessment of costs.

The characteristic record of this litigation is a chronological journal of the court's acts, in which the stages reached in each case, at every session of the court, and the terms assigned for the next stage are briefly noted: hence the name 'assignation books'. Such books contain no record of the pleading, and in my experience the outcome of a cause can rarely be known, because the sentence is not copied, unless it is abandoned, or goes to arbitration. Not all entries mention the type of cause under way, and at best one can only learn from such books the numbers of causes begun in a certain period, the names of litigants and proctors, and something about the peculiarities of court practice.

The York consistory registers beginning in 1370 and surviving continuously from the early fifteenth century, are all of this type, and this was the common form in all ecclesiastical courts by the sixteenth century, except for simple correction cases. At Ely we have one example which seems to have been introduced during the professional-isation of the court by Richard Scrope, and which, perhaps because of the small size of the diocese, includes copies of libels and even of a few sentences. For the most part however, the medieval court books surviving at Hereford, Lichfield, Rochester, and Wells, are bald assignation books and so are the books of peculiar jurisdictions which occasionally survive. Such books were compiled and kept by the registrar of the court, who would also have been responsible for preparing the acts of cause which were first required by canon 38 of the fourth Lateran council:

We ordain that as well in ordinary as in extraordinary jurisdiction the judge shall appoint either a public person [a notary public] if one can be found, or two suitable men, who shall write down all acts of the court namely citations, delays, refusals, exceptions, petitions, responses, interrogatories and confessions of witnesses, depos-itions, productions of instruments, interlocutory appeals, renunciations, conclusions, and other things which arise, setting down places, times and persons. Acts thus written are to be distributed to the parties, provided that the originals remain with the writers . . .

Here is the authority for a great archive of court papers, which, if it survived in entirety, would provide us with the working record of a medieval canonist. Only at York, so far as I am aware, has any body of the papers of a court come down from before 1500, and this is a truly great body of material, still only partly exploited.[25] It includes some of the private notes of proctors, including one concerning an advocate of the court who in 1411 was cited as defendant in a matrimonial cause, and wrote to a colleague who was evidently acting as his proctor:

Dear Brother,
I earnestly entreat you to be good enough to represent me yourself or find a good substitute, in our court next Wednesday and ask for the postponement of my business because I must be with my master. In case you cannot influence the judge in my favour have ready an exception declining the jurisdiction of the court. Also be good enough to ask Robert Ragnal's help and favour for me.
Yours,
Thomas Cleveland

The plaintiff's case was, of course, lost.[26]

With the courts of appeal in the Canterbury province we have fewer records, thanks, it appears, to the destruction of its central registry in Doctors' Commons, during the Great Fire of 1666. Fortunately two types of evidence remain to illuminate the procedure of the lower courts. Any appeal to a higher court, either provincial or papal, called for the transmission to the higher court of a full narrative of all the acts against which the plaintiff was appealing, and this has produced a number of rolls, called by some 'compiled acta'; they seem usually to be copies made for the plaintiff's case, and since they are concerned with tithe disputes, in appropriated rectories, they have passed since the Reformation into the muniments of private families as deed of title. Many such rolls appear in the Lancashire Record Office and a number of the cases can be followed through all their stages in the local consistory court, usually that of Lichfield.[27] Another such record, which I cherish, now in the Bristol Record Office (1A/6/1) is a roll of depositions belonging to a cause appealed from the consistory of Worcester to Arches. They set out in overpowering detail the boundaries between two Bristol parishes, St Michael and St Laurence, in connection with disputed tithe of a *domus latrina seu cloaca communis* near the river in Fromegate. Such depositions were probably taken locally, on commission from the official of Arches, and the execution of these commissions was a useful source of extra revenue for the personnel of the local courts.

The second type of record illuminating the activities of the higher courts is the plaintiff's copies of individual papers prepared in the course of an appeal: these are still to be found in the archives of colleges, collegiate churches, and cathedrals. Hereford Cathedral has a particularly fine set of papers of the mid fourteenth century arising from its claim to parochial rights in the city.[28] Wells Cathedral, Christ Church, Oxford, New College, Oxford, and St George's, Windsor, all have samples of activity of this sort.

Some of the York papers suggest that the proctor drew up a statement of his cause headed 'What I intend to prove' and there survives, in a binding fragment at Kendal, a list of answers to be made by a defendant's proctor in a Sussex court.[29]

The respective parts played in the conduct of any case by the advocate and proctor are not easy to determine, apart from the proctor's obligation to represent his master and the advocate's duty to advise on the way the suit is conducted. We know that from about 1239, when Drogheda declared in his *Summa aurea* that proctors should be paid, they were increasingly treated as professional lawyers.[30] At times during the fourteenth and fifteenth centuries they can be found suing former masters (that is employers), usually by a suit of *fidei lesio* (breach of faith) for the recovery of their fees, and the final stage of most causes at this period, and indeed, well into the post-Reformation period, is the taxation by the court of bills of cost for the suit. Files of such bills survive from the post-Reformation years, but are rarely seen from earlier times. One which survives as a stray document among benefice papers at Lincoln from a suit of 1439 is particularly illuminating about the way in which the proctor occupied his time.[31]

First, for an original citation from the bishop of Lincoln's audience. 8d.
Expenses of going, staying and returning from Market Deeping to seek the same. 6d.
For the mandatary's fee, and for certification of the mandate. 13d.
For a dinner for Mr. Richard Ikelon, advocate, travelling to Sleaford. 4d.
To Mr. John Clyfton for writing bonds and conditions of the same lord. 3d.
Expenses of the vicar to and from Sleaford. 2s. 6d.
Expenses of the advocate's journey to Sleaford. 6s. 8d.
Expenses of the advocate's journey to Stamford when the cause was postponed to the morrow of Holy Cross day. 4s. 11d.
For the proctor's fee at Lincoln on the Wednesday after Michaelmas. 2s. 8d.
For the commission directed to the Lord Official. 2s.
For constituting the vicar's proctor in the consistory. 2d.
For the fee for the original citation to call the Prior and convent (of Belvoir). 12d.
Paid to the Dean of Ness to execute this mandate. 6d.

Expenses of the vicar being present at the consistory at Stamford. 8d.
Fee for another citation to summon the prior and convent to appear personally
  because they dwell within the diocese of Lincoln. 12d.
Labour and expenses of the mandatary certifying the service of this citation. 3s. 4d.
Expenses of the vicar at this consistory. 6d.
Paid to the Dean of Ness for the attachment of his seal to the certificate. 4d.
Paid to the proctor for drawing up the libel. 2s.
Expenses of the vicar going and coming at this term. 10d.
To the scribe of the official for the examination of witnesses. 2s. 3d.
For the proctor's salary at the next consistory after Epiphany. 20d.
Expenses of the vicar at that term. 10d.
Expenses of the vicar at the second consistory after Candlemas. 2s.
Proctor's salary at the same term. 12d.
Expenses of the vicar at the next consistory after St Chad. 20d.
Proctor's salary at the same term. 12d.
Advocate's salary in the said cause for six consistories. 12s.
For copies of the depositions. 16d.
For the judge's fee for his execution. 2s. 8d.
Sum total £3. 3s. 9d. Assessed by the Lord to 12s 4d.

This cause was an action taken by the vicar of Tallington against the prior and convent of Belvoir who were proprietors of the rectory, for augmentation of his vicarage. In accordance with Archbishop Chichele's constitution the plaintiff was suing *in forma pauperis*.

There remains time only to consider what was the rôle of the legal expert, and especially that of the advocate, outside the sessions of the courts. It seems clear that formally and informally the advocates, and especially those attached to the courts of Canterbury who would later form Doctors' Commons, were regularly consulted, and supplied legal opinions. One such written opinion with full references to authorities, concerning a Salisbury chapter dispute, has been copied into the first act book of the chapter. It was sought from William Bateman, by this time bishop of Norwich, by his former colleague, and perhaps pupil, Thomas de Asteley. Others have been noted in formulary books, and personal memoranda, as I shall describe next week. They are, perhaps, a first tentative move towards the creation of a body of canon law reports such as Dr Baker sketched in his account of Fastolf's *Rote Decisiones*.[32]

III

The canonists' formularies

I PROPOSE TO begin by quoting part of the monumental inscription of Thomas Hearne, which seems to provide a motto for this division of my study:

> Here lieth the body of Thomas Hearne
> Who studied and preserved antiquities
> Remember the days of old
> Consider the years of many generations
> Ask thy father and he will show thee
> Thy elders and they will tell thee
> For inquire I pray thee of the former age
> And prepare thyself to the search of their fathers
> For we are but as yesterday and know nothing because our days on
>   earth are a shadow.
> Shall they not teach thee and tell thee, and utter words out of their
>   hearts?[1]

The wisdom of former ages was enshrined for the practising canon lawyer not only in the canonical texts and the multifarious commentaries on them which I have discussed in the first of these lectures, but even more in the records of procedural documents, methods of pleading, and types of cause which assiduous students copied during their apprenticeship, augmented as their careers progressed, and finally bequeathed as precious treasures to their nephews and clerks – the formularies, that is to say, which figure very prominently among the records of the church courts of the later middle ages.

In discussing the beginnings of the use of notaries public in English ecclesiastical circles Christopher Cheney cited the rubric of chapter 38 of the Fourth Lateran council: *Consuetudo loci facit instrumentum authenticum*;[2] local custom, that is to say, confers authenticity on an instrument, as proof of the varieties of local custom to which notaries trained in the civil and canon law in Italy would have had to accustom themselves when first they practised in England. Such public persons became indispensable when during the twelfth century the entire western church adopted procedure by written record in its courts, and a skilful public person licensed to draw up and authenticate the official documents was increasingly needed. Appeals to Rome, and the employment of judges delegate to hear the cases, had at a fairly early stage called for guides to the conduct of proceedings and the documents called for, and Dr Sayers and Professor Logan have described judge-delegate formularies devised for this purpose.[3] In addition, judicial centres in the English church soon developed their own peculiar methods of preparing and presenting cases, as B.Z. Kedar has pointed out,[4] and it was partly to equip clerks to plead in these courts, and to draw up documents required for the conduct of cases, that informal collections, also known as formularies, were made in the fourteenth and fifteenth centuries.

Walter Stapeldon, bishop of Exeter from 1308–26, a well-known Oxford canonist who established the college later to be called Exeter, and a civil servant who was murdered by a London mob, had investigated the arrangements of his own consistory, as we have seen, and laid down regulations for the examination of witnesses and the behaviour of advocates. His successor John Grandisson promulgated statutes for the consistory as his contemporary Henry Burghersh did for Lincoln. For the court of Canterbury a series of rules for officers was initiated in 1295 by Archbishop Winchelsey; modifications and amplifications to these were made by John Stratford in 1342, and by William Courtenay.[5] The concern of all these statutes or regulations is as much the custom and style of the courts as conformity with the canon law. Those intending to practise in these courts found it useful to have copies of the statutes to hand, usually in a private note book or formulary. Trinity College Cambridge manuscript 397 (B.16.34) provides a fifteenth century example of this type: it contains copies of the statutes of Winchelsey and Stratford, with notes on divergent practices and a series of later additions on modes of appeal to Arches. Professor Logan is preparing an edition of the Canterbury statutes and will discuss them thoroughly, so I shall say no more about them here.

The formularies had other contents, however, besides these statutes of courts, and it is time to consider in greater detail how they came about, for what purposes they were used, and where they are now to be found. The evidence of wills suggests that they originated as personal compilations which passed as bequests to nephews and associates who augmented and amplified them in accordance with their own needs and probably also passed them on again in their own wills. On occasion they seem to have been sold on the open market, like the manuscript, now All Souls ms. 182, which had been purchased before

1500 by William Elyot rector of Blackawton. Perhaps the earliest clear reference to a formulary of our type is to be found in the will of William Doune, Archdeacon of Leicester, which is itself copied into a formulary of which we shall hear more. Doune, who began his official professional life as a notary public in Bishop Grandisson's service, about 1361, bequeathed to Mr Richard Medmenham the use for life, with reversion to Osney Abbey, of 'a large thick book containing many questions and allegations of advocates in causes heard in the Curia', and to Thomas Pepir, notary public, who was evidently his personal registrar and scribe, his silver pen and inkhorn and

a quire covered with white leather containing commissions issuing from the court of Rome, propositions, articles, and much other useful matter written almost entirely with my own hand, and containing in part a membrane of parchment where are written letters of commission and other letters of bishops and certain other things which I got together in my youth when I was in the service of the Bishop of Exeter.[6]

Robert of Austhorpe, a Lincolnshire clerk with Balliol connections, in 1373 bequeathed to his clerk Henry Welle 'all my acts, with a repertory to them which is at present at Balliol Hall'.[7] The inventory of John Trefnant bishop of Hereford, who died in 1404, included several of these compilations: 'one big formulary with various forms of letters . . . A smaller paper book covered with red leather containing various questions [this may of course have been an academic record], a paper book of decisions of the Rota and other doubtful decisions and allegations of the same Bishop'.[8] One wonders whether Thomas Felde, dean of Hereford, who died in 1419, inherited some of these from Trefnant, for he bequeathed in his will 'all his books and quires of the faculties of civil and canon law, and his quire of letters sent'.[9] Scattered references continue: Robert Alne, examiner general of the court of York, in 1440 left to the Cambridge University Library 'a paper book with tractates and the conclusions of the Rota, as well as Pope John XXII's Extravagants', and Robert Esyngwald, a proctor of the court of York, in 1443 bequeathed to Mr William Langton, once his clerk, 'all my books of the practice of the court, namely libels, positions, articles, exceptions and so on'.[10]

Many of the books so passing from hand to hand must have originated with English practitioners in the court of Rome, such as those to whom Professor Jacob devoted some detailed study, and especially those like William Swan, who instructed his proctor Robert Ely to keep safe for him, in his absence in England, '*Decisiones Rote*, bound up with other tracts, a formulary of *Audiencie Contradictarum*, the rules of the papal chancery, a quire of supplications, and a quire of medicines'.[11]

A number of the bequests relate to compilations arising from the testator's own practice, as we have seen, and perhaps stayed in or near the church courts with which their compiler was associated. The diocesan records of Salisbury, Lincoln, and Ely still contain considerable collections of such material. There are thirty-three formularies at Salisbury, many of the earlier of which are not apparently concerned with practice in the Salisbury courts. Lincoln and Ely each have twenty-four, while the archiepiscopal archives at York include forty-nine such volumes, mostly drawn from York sources. Similar groups are known at Durham, Exeter, and Lichfield, and with the Cambridge University Archives. Almost all of the purely local collections date from the middle of the sixteenth century or later and most have a more-or-less formal arrangement, often alphabetically entered under such heads as articles, certificates, citations, commissions, decrees, libels, responses. Names of parties, proctors, and places are often omitted, although the court and its judges are usually entered.[12] All told, such compilations are best treated in my fourth lecture, but there are a few related medieval examples, some of them more irregular in format, and certainly of greater importance to our present inquiry. At Lincoln, for example, there is a handsomely written volume (Form. 23) which was plainly compiled by an official of the courts of Canterbury, perhaps Richard Brinkcley, examiner general and later dean of Arches during the first part of Chichele's archiepiscopate (1414–43). There are at Ely two York formularies (EDR F5/32 and 33) which are closely associated with John Newton, official of York, and Stephen Scrope, archdeacon of Richmond, and another York volume of much the same time had migrated to Lincoln before 1500, and is now Cambridge University Library Additional ms. 3115. York itself has a formulary of documents associated with the Archbishop Alexander Neville (1374–88) which has always been treated as a register (York Borthwick Institute register 13). The University Archives in Cambridge include a late medieval volume, classified as Coll. Admin. 39, which seems to originate in a notarial practice based on Cambridge active during the first forty years of the sixteenth century, and serving the archdeaconry and diocese of Ely, the university, colleges, and religious houses in the town, and, on occasion, the sacrist of Bury. It appears to be associated with Geoffrey Glynn, of Bishop West's *familia*, but I have not succeeded in isolating any single compiler.[13]

Most medieval formularies escaped from official custody, if they were ever in it, and into the collections of individuals, and this is a topic I shall look at again in the fourth lecture. There are a number of such compilations in Oxford and Cambridge colleges. Corpus Christi College, Cambridge, ms. 170, the notebook of an early sixteenth century notary public Nicholas Collys, who was associated with the College of Stoke by Clare, may well have entered the library along with the other books of Matthew Parker, who had been master of the Stoke College. The Queen's College, Oxford, ms. 54, with which I shall deal in greater detail below, a Colchester/London book, was evidently in the hands of Sir Robert Cotton at one time, but was acquired by Robert Eglesfield, who presumably gave it to the college. I have made no attempt at an exhaustive survey, but there is no doubt that the best and largest group is that in the Harleian manuscripts, which was assembled by Edward Stillingfleet, bishop of Worcester, from whose executors it was purchased by Robert Harley in 1699.[14]

I should like first to consider a formulary book of a type which is, I believe, a unique survival: this is the book of Mr John Lydford, an Oxford canonist who was successively advocate of the court of Canterbury, official of William of Wykeham, and archdeacon of Totnes. The volume passed after his death in 1407 to his clerk James Carslegh, who became official of Exeter and who added a number of pages to it before his own death. After Carslegh's death the volume seems to have remained with the Exeter records, where it is still to be found. Some fourteen years ago I edited Lydford's portion for the Devon and Cornwall record society.[15] Lydford was a canonist and ecclesiastical administrator at a time when such men were leaders in their own world and his memorandum book records, naturally and unconsciously, the preoccupations of his long life, while providing examplars for the future of a variety of ecclesiastical and legal forms. The arrangement is not strictly chronological, but we see Lydford first in Oxford, where he was still a student, taking some part in the causes in the Chancellor's court and at the same time listening to and recording the *questiones* of leading canonists such as Ralph Tregrisiou and John and Baldwin Shillingford. He passed on from Oxford to the court of Canterbury, all this time in the service of, and under the patronage of his fellow Devonian William Courtenay, who was bishop of Hereford and London and eventually archbishop of Canterbury. It was Courtenay who condemned the heresies of Wycliffe and his followers in a council at London in 1382, where Lydford served as an assessor: his memorandum book records the proceedings of this council at some length, along with other later Lollard materials. Much of Lydford's book is taken up with legal notes of a professional nature: he shows clearly how by a series of exceptions an opponent could profit from procedural errors in the presentation of a case. Appeals to the court of Canterbury could begin, he demonstrates, by *querela*, *provocacio*, or *suggestio*. Confessions and *sentencie diffinitive* are invalid unless they include certain specific information. A dissatisfied plaintiff might refuse to obey a judge on the grounds of his bias, and this could afford sufficient reason for an appeal to a higher court (nos. 146–7). A *consultacio* is the right way to treat a writ of prohibition (127), and specialised advice, in an *informacio* or counsel's opinion, is often necessary in the problems of a visitation court. One such *informacio*, drawn up by himself, about a proposal for the establishment of a collegiate church, is disarmingly marked '*Bona*' and contains a number of characteristic brief quotations from the decretum, Hostiensis, John Andreas, Otto's constitution *Cum sit ars*, and Ottobuono's *de presumcionibus*. All told, Lydford's chief preoccupations were with the episcopal courts of audience and consistory; the documents which he copies for transmission to Arches, or for appeals to the curia, show no sign that he was personally involved as advocate or proctor in Avignon or Rome.

No other formulary known to me has so marked a personal quality as this but there is a handful of other specimens which are certainly more informative and more individual than the sort of non-committal collection which I have described from Lincoln. The earliest in time is now in the Northampton Archives Office with the Peterborough diocesan records, (Misc. Bk 1), where it was first observed and partially described by Hamilton Thompson. It was subsequently exploited by H.E. Salter for Oxford material and it was Salter who decided to attribute it to John Snappe, another Oxford, Exeter, and Winchester official, who had also been an advocate of the court of Canterbury.[16] Snappe's name occurs in one or two places in the book, and he was certainly associated with some at least of the documents in causes appealed to Arches. At the same time, however, there is a good deal of material from the consistory of London, and from the archdeaconry of Westminster Abbey, which seems to be the work not of Snappe, but of William de Stuyecle, who was also an advocate of Arches, and of Richard Brynkeley, examiner general of the same court. Much of the material seems to be compiled from the papers of one or more advocates whose opinions are noted after the material of appeal is copied. The whole book has a 'Canterbury' bias and this is particularly demonstrated by a group of letters addressed to cardinals, with other notes about the council of Pisa, which seem to be related to the transaction of 1408–9, discussed by E.F. Jacob, in which the leading figures are Brynkeley and John Perche.[17] One might suggest that the volume was compiled in London in the office of a group of notaries and advocates who served the courts of Canterbury, the central courts of the diocese of London, and some London-based peculiar juris-dictions.

The next formulary I want to consider is BL Harleian ms. 862, which was once in Stillingfleet's hands. In the first half of the fifteenth century it was in the registry of the archdeaconries of Totnes and Exeter, and from it G.G. Coulton took the record of an archidiaconal visitation of 1443, which he published in the *English Historical Review*.[18] The collection seems to have been carried to Totnes by Robert Stephyn, notary public of the diocese of Exeter, who was associated with Lydford's former clerk James Carslegh, by this time archdeacon of Totnes. Stephyn was in Oxford at times, and in 1424 took part in the service of an inhibition, the inherent dangers of which he demonstrated. He approached Mr William Wenlock and Mr Robert Woller at the north door of St Mary the Virgin and said to them *in vulgari*: 'Mayster I moste serve yow as I have served your fellowes: by the autorite of this mandement I inhibitt yow' and a certain Mr William Grenewod, advancing with angry expression *et vultu protervo*, laid hands on him, dragged him by the arm saying: 'Come thens ye owe not to obey his mandement' and finally cried out to the unfortunate Stephyn 'Lewde Jak go pysse the with thy man-dement.'

The documents recorded by Stephyn are mostly notarial com-positions chiefly from the early practice of Chichele, Walter Medford, and William Lyndewode, and are drawn from West Country and Welsh sources. Their main interest seems to be the form and conduct of appeals to the provincial courts. They cite authorities freely, such as '*Novellas constituciones dispendiosam* and *sepe*. Clem 1c.2', John Andreas on procedure, the provincial constitutions of Boniface and Stratford, and Exeter synodal statutes. In one case at least, alternative methods of presenting a matrimonial cause, as practised in the archdeaconry of Oxford and the consistory of London, are quoted. The collection seems to be predominantly notarial and is arranged coherently in alphabetical order of types of document, but it is possible to detect some preoccupation with certain contemporary issues such as matrimonial disputes, episcopal dilapidations, and burial fees. This may perhaps be another example of rudimentary law reporting.

The next book to be discussed, which is now in the Rochester diocesan records (Dr b 010), is essentially a Canterbury/Arches/London book. It was quoted several times by Miss Churchill and Mr Emden, and the revisers of Le Neve's *Fasti* have also referred to it, but it has not been systematically described or exploited. It is based on the re-arrangement of files of papers in causes appealed to Arches, documents from which recur throughout the book. The advocates/proctors represented are two, or perhaps three, men named Cole, all of the diocese of Norwich, and presumably relations: Mr John Cole LL B, proctor general and advocate of Arches, commissary of London and prebendary of Caddington in St Paul's, Mr James Cole senior notary public, also a St Paul's prebendary, who had died before 1439, and James Cole junior, also notary public. All lived in London; many of the notarial documents are dated from the house of James Cole senior, in St Gregory's parish, and this was evidently the centre of the legal practice. James Cole senior calls himself at one time 'scribe of William Lyndwode'. Apart from Arches appeals, which included a long and important cause brought by the parish of Wymondham against visitation by the diocesan, and another by the parishioners of Lesness (Kent) against the appropriators of the benefice, members of the group acted regularly for the hospitals of Bedlam and St Bartholomew in Smithfield, for the two Charterhouses in London and at Sheen, and for the newly founded Bridgettine house of Sion. They record a number of notable compositions achieved by Bishop Alnwick and of outstanding *sententie diffinitive* pronounced by William Lyndwode, *facile princeps*, but the main emphasis of the volume is notarial. Actual documents executed by James Cole senior are fastened into the cover, there are notes on the calculation of dates, lists of moveable feasts, memoranda about the use of authentic seals on a proxy, and a long series of proxies and certifications of ecclesiastical processes. One of James Cole senior's documents, written 'in a low chamber recently constructed near the abbot's great chamber at Bermondsey', records an ordination made by Abbot Thomas Tetford, just before his death, about observances to be made at the death of members of the house. Part of the front cover of the book is a public instrument in which the executors of Mr John Snappe are parties, and this may well explain the presence in a nearby office of the Peterborough volume later to be associated with Snappe.

The Queen's College, Oxford, manuscript which I have already mentioned as having been once in the hands of Sir Robert Cotton, is another compilation from a notarial practice which is essentially London based, and which may owe its core material to John Derby, notary public, scribe of the official of Arches (1459), and to Mr Edmund Derby, official of Colchester, who was presumably his connection. It is less obviously a purely notarial compilation than the Rochester book and its earlier sections, from Cambridge, Ely, and Huntingdon, in some ways parallel with Lydford's personal record, are concerned with the preoccupations of a young student of law qualifying himself for higher things. He was maintaining himself to some degree by notarial practice, especially on behalf of friends attempting to acquire benefices. The later pages are reflections of the activities of Derby and his associates in the courts of Canterbury and in the day-to-day business of the diocese of London: Richard Combe, advocate of the consistory of London, figures constantly in this section.

In this administrative section a notary might be called on to draw up a resignation deed, draft an appeal for an executor sensible of mistreatment, write an instrument embodying a confession of matrimony, draft an arbitration in a tithe dispute, and serve an inhibition on John Berners, goldsmith in Cheapside, who replied 'I recke not of thine inhibition for I have a sentence, signed and sealled and under a notary signe.' The documents concerning appeals to Arches are particularly varied and interesting, though there is no time to look at more than one or two. I rather like the appeal of a literate layman, John Brew of St Dunstan in the West, against the sentence of John London, a monk of Westminster and commissary of the archdeacon of Westminster, in a cause of defamation brought against him by Geoffrey B., fletcher. There is something attractive, too, about an appeal, on complaint of a proctor, against a criminal prosecution brought by Mr Thomas Ruggeley, commissary of London, against Lora Rekes, a woman of London, for adultery with *quodam clericatore armorum Scotorum herawe vulgariter nuncupato*. Intermittently there are memoranda set down by the copyist to remind himself of an interesting point: 'nota hic de examinacione testium et in quibus debent examinari quando agitur de consanguinate et affinitate Que sunt hec necessaria notat Hostiensis in lectura in c.licet ex quadam . . . super verbo habere'.

Towards the end of the book there are notes on how to calculate the indiction, which in England always changes on the seventh of the kalends of October, but in the Roman curia and other places at the feast of Christmas. There is an index of topics towards the end of this section which is followed by copies of the statutes of Winchelsey and Meopham for the court of Arches. There is also a heavily annotated transcript of the text of the Sext, with the gloss of John Andreas *in ordinario*. All these seem to date from Edmund Derby's student days, which also produced, it seems, the notes about appeals which occur in the earlier folios of the book: 'No appeal lies from the archdeacon or his official directly to the court of Canterbury. Why? Because it is a middle court (*medium*). Devolution never ought to be done except in the failure of an inferior judge to act.'

Perhaps for this audience, and certainly for myself, the glimpses afforded of the Ely consistory and its related courts are among the most interesting parts of the book. It is possible to re-assemble, under various heads in the text, all the stages in a cause of *fidei lesio* concerning misappropriation of two loads of thack contracted to another person. The appropriators of Great St Mary in Cambridge (King's Hall) sue the churchwardens in the archdeacon's court for their failure to repair the nave. Mr John Newton, official of Ely in 1419, testifies, with a view of ordination I fancy, to the good life and conversation of W.B., a literate brought up in a grammar school and then employed by the parishioners of Holy Trinity, Cambridge, as a holy-water carrier. William de Okham (?Oakham), a scholar in the university, testifies to a marriage he had celebrated, with the vicar's permission, in the Church of St Mary outside Trumpington Gates (Little St Mary). The official of Ely requires the rector of St Vigor, Fulbourne to exhibit in court the muniments he holds for the free chapel within the curia of JC in his parish. The vice chancellor and bedells certify to the official in 1468 that they have duly cited John Hudson and John Marley, parish clerks of Histon, and scholars of the university. I could go on for ever; this is an unusually rich source of material which I have seen recorded nowhere else.

The book obviously remained of practical use and continued to receive fresh entries until 1531, when it was in the hands of clerks associated with St Paul's, who copied in extracts from the cathedral muniments and a Privy Council decree about a contract between two Florentine merchants. The last mark of ownership is on the cover, where the name 'Master Doctor Bellessez' occurs in the same hand as a note about wine: 'hec quinque probantur forcia, formosa, fragrantia, frigida, frisa'. This man may well be Anthony Belasyse, BCL Cambridge 1520, and subsequently LL D of a foreign University, Master in Chancery and prebendary of Lincoln, Wells, and York.

One final compilation worth examination is that held in the University Archives (Coll. Admin. 39). Its compilers are not easy to trace. Geoffrey Glynn certainly provided Welsh documents, but Robert Clyff features throughout as a proctor and advocate, and three notaries, Edward Haynes and John Hosyer of Cambridge and Nicholas Collys of St Faith, London (the compiler of the Corpus collection) are all represented. The period covered runs from 1501 to 1562, and the documents emanate partly from the Chancellor's court and the university (admissions, and resignations of scholars and fellows, a charge of dilapidation against JW principal of Burdon Hostel and two fellows, a decree concerning the proctorial election of 1542–3), and partly from the consistory of Ely. The parishioners of St Clement are ordered to repair their roof, pavement, vestments, and church furniture. A letter of proxy of the Ely clergy meeting in synod at Barnwell in 1529 for the forthcoming Convocation ends 'Datum apud Bawdie Barnwell'. The official is requested by the deputy Vice Chancellor, Thomas Thurlby, to cite JS of Fulbourne St Vigor, a layman, to answer William Branbe clerk and scholar. He certifies that EC of the vill of E in the Isle of Ely is a genuine sufferer from falling sickness and therefore worthy to receive alms in aid of a pilgrimage in search of a cure and he testifies to the taking of an oath by another man to visit the Holy Land, 'and we saw his breast marked with an iron cross alight'. As usual this volume attracted the idle scribbles of the notaries and their clerks and it ends:

> Balow balow balowle lowla low
> By the window blaus the blud from me ballew.

All of the formularies I have discussed have some family resemblance, and I cherished for a long time the belief that one might find an exemplar from which they all derive, or at least a common source on which they relied. However, I hope that my examination of these examples serves to show that there is no common stock. It is clear that some at least, and especially the Rochester and Lincoln examples, were compiled during the archiepiscopate of Chichele, but that is the furthest that one dare go. I can find no evidence that more than one of the books include a copy of the same leading judgment: each compiler made his own selection from what he had to hand. For the rest, they are almost all an amalgam of notarial and canonistic knowledge. They combine, that is to say, examples for the guidance of notaries who must draft documents but they also report important judgments, *sententie diffinitive*, and compositions resulting from arbitrations by leading lawyers, as well as outstanding opinions on causes, *informaciones*, that is to say. John Lydford's book and Harleian mss. 862 reflect the predominance of Mr John Shillingford who was a native of the diocese of Exeter and several of whose *informaciones* can be read here. He was, as the Lydford book clearly shows, a member of the circle surrounding William Courtenay, with which Lydford himself was closely associated. Lydford also repeated important judgments by Richard Scrope, official of Ely, and later archbishop of York.

Harleian ms. 862 reflects the association of Walter Medford with William Lyndwode, and the Rochester book is even more clearly under Lyndwode's influences. The Queen's College, Oxford, manuscript includes some sentences of Dr John Newton and Mr William Oakham, officials of Ely, but is not so concerned with outstanding legal opinions as the earlier volumes.

It seems reasonable to suggest that most of the formularies examined here are dominated by the wisdom and experience of the advocates practising in the courts of Canterbury and by their disciples and connections in the West Country, with a single example from eastern England, the Queen's College, Oxford, manuscript. At the same time it is fair to remark that there was a similar strong tradition associated with the courts of York which produced three collections now here in Cambridge, two in the Ely diocesan records, and one in the University Library's collections. All these York examples are more formal and workmanlike than the Canterbury specimens. With a few exceptions (John Newton as official of York), the documents are anonymous, there are no outstanding 'presentations' such as appear in the Canterbury examples, and even the larger of the Ely volumes has little unusual matter, apart from that troublesome Ely Lollard document referred to in print by Alfred Gibbons almost a century ago, which has haunted my steps ever since I first administered the Ely records. All things considered, these York specimens are no more than routine compilations and the contents of ULC Add. 3115 are particularly revealing in this regard. The *repertorium* which covers folios 34 and 35 includes these entries:

citation about transcripts of instruments and other letters
citation about a petition for a bull concerning augmentation of a vicarage
citation (first) made by papal delegates about augmentation

citation (second)
citation (third) by public announcement obtained *sub mutue vicissitudine*
citation to show cause why a party defending an appeal should not be dismissed
    because the appellant did not prosecute the cause on the appointed day
letters to the chapter of York, the Archdeaconry of Richmond, the chapter of
    Beverley and the Custos of Howden, concerning the convocation of York.

I remain convinced that most of these books are essentially the compilations of notaries learning their trade during their early days in the courts, as William Doune did in the courts of Exeter. If they were not immediately regarded as guides to the practice of the registries and courts they almost certainly took on that function as they passed into other hands. Only for short periods, and in a few cases, do they incorporate direct examples of academic teaching and only intermittently can they be regarded as (canon) law reports. There is no doubt that the practitioners in the *Rota sacri palatii* were more dedicated professional lawyers than any officer of a diocesan or provincial consistory, who might be, and was, required to write and issue all sorts of administrative documents, as the York list suggests. Even the officials, advocates, and proctors of the courts of Canterbury might find themselves recording resignations of benefices, papal licenses for questors, appeals against the assessment of subsidies, and proclamations of papal jubilees. Because of this 'mixed' function, the English medieval canonists' formularies are only intermittently law reports, though they often take on the character of vade mecum handbooks which they are to assume almost entirely in the post-Reformation period.

IV

Post-Reformation literature: collectors and practical applications

I SHALL BE concerned in this lecture with a complicated series of investigations, none of which can be treated so fully as I could wish: perhaps the whole series should have been devoted to these topics. I want first of all to look at the place and practical application of canonistic literature in the church courts, and the range and importance of its survival there. I must then turn briefly to the place of such literature in the collections which survive, or of which we have record. There is finally the developing historiography of the uses of canon law studies, from the application of it made by Selden, through the antiquarian studies and high-church sympathies of the later seventeenth century to the revival of an interest never completely dead, by sympathisers with the Oxford Movement, its culmination in Bishop Stubbs, and its re-definition in Cambridge by F.W. Maitland.

The Cromwellian injunctions of 1535, which forbade the study of the canon law in the universities, must seem to have cut the church courts from the source of their authority.[1] The gap thus created was for the next twenty-five years expected to be filled by the issue by the Crown of a new code of law. Meanwhile the church courts continued to sit: at York, for example, there is no gap in the series of consistory court registers. Judges heard causes, wills were proved, proctors represented suitors, but soon practical measures were called for to maintain the supply of qualified personnel to the courts. In 1545 an Act of Parliament empowered doctors of the civil law to exercise ecclesiastical jurisdiction,[2] and thus created a class of church lawyers who until the middle of the nineteenth century remained outside the common law of the realm. The courts in which they pleaded and judged, in addition to the archidiaconal and diocesan consistories, the surviving peculiar jurisdictions, and the provincial courts of Canterbury and York, were the courts of admiralty and chivalry, which had always provided a few examples in the medieval formularies, and in the new economic bustle of the sixteenth century now became far busier, and the new high court of Delegates, which after 1534 became the court of appeal for all civil law causes, including those from church

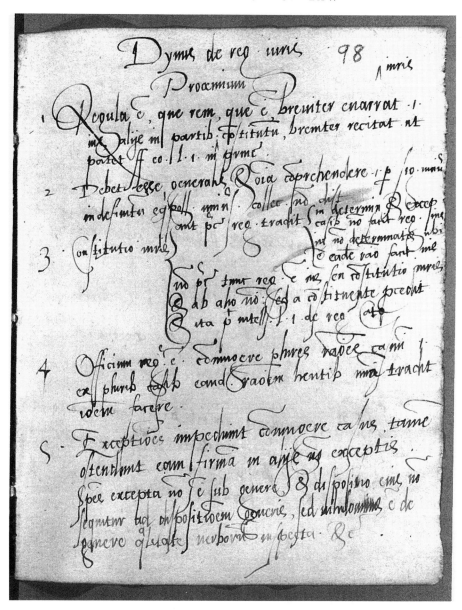

Fig. 6 Notes of Thomas Legge from Dinus, *de regulis iuris*, late sixteenth century (EDR F5/49)

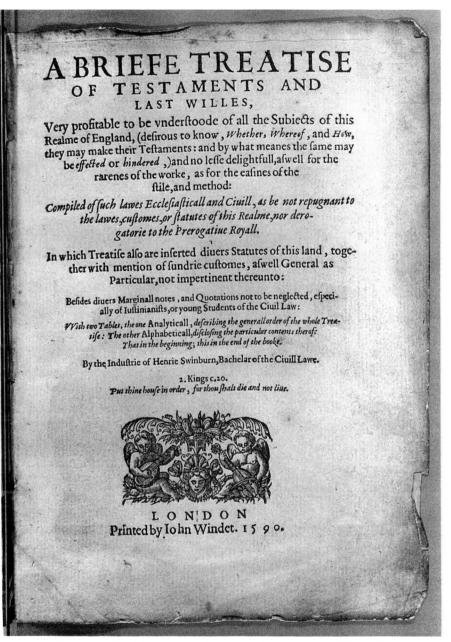

A BRIEFE TREATISE
OF TESTAMENTS AND
LAST WILLES,

Very profitable to be vnderstoode of all the Subiects of this
Realme of England, (desirous to know , *Whether, Whereof* , and *How*,
they may make their Testaments : and by what meanes the same may
be *effected* or *hindered* ,)and no lesse delightfull,aswell for the
rarenes of the worke, as for the easines of the
stile, and method:

*Compiled of such lawes Ecclesiasticall and Ciuill , as be not repugnant to
the lawes,customes,or statutes of this Realme,nor dero-
gatorie to the Prerogatiue Royall.*

In which Treatise also are inserted diuers Statutes of this land , together with mention of sundrie customes, aswell General as
Particular,not impertinent thereunto:

Besides diuers Marginall notes , and Quotations not to be neglected , especially of Iustinianists,or young Students of the Ciuil Law :

With two Tables, the one Analyticall *, describing the generall order of the whole Treatise :* The other Alphabeticall,*disclosing the particular contents thereof:
That in the beginning; this in the end of the booke.*

By the Industrie of Henrie Swinburn,Bachelar of the Ciuill Lawe.

2. Kings c.20.
Put thine house in order , for thou shalt die and not liue.

LONDON
Printed by Iohn Windet. 1590.

Fig. 7 H. Swinburne, *Briefe treatise of testaments and last willes*,
London 1590

courts whence appeal previously lay to Rome.[3] Side by side with the Delegates for the eighty years after 1559 went the High Commission for Ecclesiastical Causes, which partly shared its personnel and which handled much business resulting from the controversial ecclesiastical measures of Charles I and Laud.[4]

The number of civil lawyers required was never large, and as Mr Squibb has demonstrated in his study of Doctors' Commons, where those serving the Canterbury and London courts tended to congregate, they served impartially in all the civil law courts.[5] By this time, too, relatively few of them were university trained lawyers, although most of them had had a first degree, which had preceded an apprenticeship to the notariate and practical training in the courts. For the use of such men specific guides to the intricacies of the law soon began to appear and examples have survived in some numbers. A recent study of defamation and sexual slander, written by J.A. Sharpe,[6] quotes a good example of the guides to this growing field of litigation, in John March's work, *Actions for slander or a methodicall collection under certain grounds of heads of what words are actionable in the law, and what not?* which appeared in 1647. An even busier field of litigation is that of probate business where, as early as 1590, Henry Swinburne provided in his *Brief treatise of testaments and last willes* what has been called by a recent writer 'the only textbook of English canon law in the tradition of the international body of jurists'. It is, unusually, written in English and has an appealing account of its purpose, in the foreword to the reader:[7]

Great and wonderful is the number of the manifolde writers of the Civill and Ecclesiasticall lawes, and so huge is the multitude of their sundrie sorts of bookes, as lectures, councels, tracts, decisions, questions, disputations, repetitions, cautels, clausels, common opinions, singulars, contradictions, concordances, methodes, summes, practickes, tables, repertories and bookes of other kindes (apparent monuments of their endlesse and invincible labours) that in my conceite, it is impossible for any man to read over the hundred part of their works though living an hundred yeeres he did intende none other worke. Wherfore by the publishing of this testamentarie treatise, I may be thought to powre water into the see, to carrie owles to Athens and to trouble the reader with a matter altogether needlesse and superfluous: But yet for all this, in case this one little booke may serve instead of many great volumes, then I hope that in the equal judgement of such as be indifferently affected the same is rather to be admitted as commodious then rejected as superfluous.

At the same time Swinburne's summary of the fields he intends to cover is as clear and distinct as one could wish:

I thought it not onely not superfluous but expedient for this common wealth to make collection of the most principall lawes Civill and Ecclesiasticall, perteining to testaments made before the xxv yeare of King Henrie the eight, I meane of those civill lawes which bee not contrarie to the Ecclesiasticall lawes and of these Ecclesiasticall lawes which bee not any waye prejudiciall or hurtfull to the prerogative royall, nor repugnant to the lawes, statutes, or customes of this realm: but agreeing peacably amongest themselves, and as shaking handes together like friends, and like loving brethren, saluting and embracing each other, may now still be executed as they were before the making of the saide act. Amongest which lawes Civill and Ecclesiasticall, I thought good likewise (as just occasion should be offered and as the opportunitie of the place fitted) to insert such statutes of this realme, and to make mention of such custome as well generall as particular as be not impertinent thereunto.

More usually, the literature provided for the lawyers and clergy was of a more pedestrian and rigidly practical variety, in much the same spirit as the summaries William of Pagula had prepared for the use of simple priests, as described by Professor Boyle. Perhaps the earliest of these, and that most widely disseminated, was the Praxis prepared by Francis Clerke, chiefly for the London and Canterbury courts. This circulated very widely in manuscript (there are copies in the Ely diocesan and University Archives), before it was published in 1666. A similar work was Henry Conset's *Practice of the spiritual or ecclesiastical courts* which appeared in 1681. Clerke's work was re-issued with additions by Thomas Oughton in 1738, as *Ordo iudiciorum sive methodus procedendi in negotiis et litibus in foro ecclesiastico-civili*, in which it is interesting to find him citing a work *De ordine judiciorum* which had been published at Venice by Maranti in 1578.

Meanwhile John Godolphin had issued in 1678 an abridgment of the law, *Repertorium canonicum* and John Ayliffe a similar work, *Parergon iuris canonici Anglicani*, which was published in 1726. The place of these would-be standard works was taken in most libraries, especially those of the higher clergy (my own copy is the subscription copy of James Yorke, then dean of Lincoln, and later bishop of Ely), by Richard Burn's two volumes on *Ecclesiastical Law* which first appeared in 1763, and was reprinted many times. It is an alphabetical dictionary in the best medieval tradition, and is very well documented. The article on *acolyte* for example, begins with references to Lyndwode and cites White Kennett, Gibson, and Ayliffe. In his second volume Burn included a table of the provincial and legatine constitutions. From this time on Burn held the field, was many times reprinted, and very widely dispersed.

Practical lawyers did not rely solely on short cuts such as these. An opinion given by Swinburne on a tithe cause between 1601 and 1610, and now in Durham, cites the Sext and Clementines and the usual late medieval glosses, as well as demonstrating the depth of his reading in post-medieval continental works.[8] Another seventeenth-century lawyer, Robert Redmayne of the diocese of Norwich, in an opinion on the claim of Wymondham to exemption from episcopal visitation, which was copied by Anthony Harison, the bishop's secretary, cites Abbas, and the Extravagants.[9] It would be interesting to know whether he was familiar with the litigation on the same topic which is recorded in the Cole compilation now at Rochester. Other evidence of the width of post-Reformation legal reading is provided by a list of books entered on a blank flyleaf in an early-seventeenth-century legal common-place book used by the clerks in the University registry, and now among the University archives (Coll. Admin. 38); it is possibly intended as a library list of some sort and is fairly miscellaneous. The numerous legal texts include Lyndwode, Panormitanus, the Corpus Iuris, Marcellus' *de modo articulandi*, *Summa Aurea Armilli* (that is Fumus), Tractatus Guidonis Pape's *de appellacionibus*, Dynes *de regulis iuris*, and Swinburnes *de testamentis*.

Individual lawyers employed in the church courts show their acquaintance with such recondite works as these, and others in occasional memoranda and drafts. James Tabor, for example, who was active as both university registrary and diocesan registrar in the first half of the seventeenth century was clearly acquainted, as we might expect him to be, with all the standard texts of his own and earlier days.[10] It is perhaps more surprising to find similar evidence of reading in the recently published journal of Henry Prescott, deputy registrar at Chester in the early eighteenth century, and an LL B of Trinity College, Dublin. On 18 June 1704, being at home, indisposed, he solaced himself by reading Durandus' *de consecracione*. In the next month he consulted and quoted Carranza's *Summa consiliorum* (1549–1600) and read Durandus' *de libellis*. There is one occasion when Prescott and the chancellor of the diocese, John Wainwright, 'discourse of the canon law in the coffee-house'.[11]

One final source of knowledge for the routine legal official was the type of compilation we have already discussed in the third lecture. Here the quantity of material is overpowering, for it is clear that individual lawyers sought out such material even when they might be constructing their own. Prescott recorded that a visiting lawyer was in Chester and in the coffee-house 'inquired after old praxes in our way'.

The groups of such praxes still surviving in diocesan registries show that there must have been a ready market for them, and that their custodians/owners consulted and annotated them freely. Even so old a collection as Lydford's has on its flyleaf in a seventeenth-century hand: '*Vide libellum recusatorium* infra in fo.1v.' and many later examples can be found with annotations and indexes made by owners. It is true that the historian of the Gloucester courts, F.S. Hockaday, an earnest and painstaking scholar, and also a practising lawyer, suggested that by the sixteenth century the *praxes* are copied from each other and are fossilised,[12] but this has not been my experience, and certainly the acquisition of samples from outside the diocese continued well into the eighteenth century. One might indeed postulate some sort of exchange and mart, operating perhaps in the vicinity of Doctors' Commons. The Salisbury formularies include samples from London/Canterbury and Norwich; a manuscript copy of Clerke is bound up with one of them. The York collection has samples from London, Chichester, Ely, and Canterbury. At Ely the examples range more widely, with Salisbury, Lincoln, and London collections, a set of Durham statutes, two versions of Clerke and many sets of court papers (broken files, one imagines) from diverse sources throughout the southern province, which have been sorted by type, stitched, and bound up as home-made formularies. Many of these Ely formularies bear on their flyleaves the name of Denis L'Isle, who proceeded LL B in 1712, was deputy diocesan registrar, and auditor and registrar of Trinity College. L'Isle, about whom I can discover no other information, must have ranged fairly widely to acquire this collection. A similar figure was the antiquarian-minded Thomas Sympson, deputy registrar in Lincoln in the middle of the eighteenth century, who himself put together one or two of the surviving Lincoln samples.[13]

We have now reached a stage in our consideration of the literature of the canon law when library lists and probate inventories allow us to see how many Cambridge scholars at any one time acquired and owned, or had access to, the texts and commentaries of the canon law. Where those books came from to go into private or public collections it is not now easy to say. Some must have been purchased abroad, in Paris or Amsterdam, others may have come into the stationers' shops in London or Cambridge, and Sturbridge Fair perhaps offered a convenient place for the selling and picking-up of rarities. There must of course have remained in Cambridge a number of pre-Reformation printed books circulating among dealers, or stored awaiting purchase,

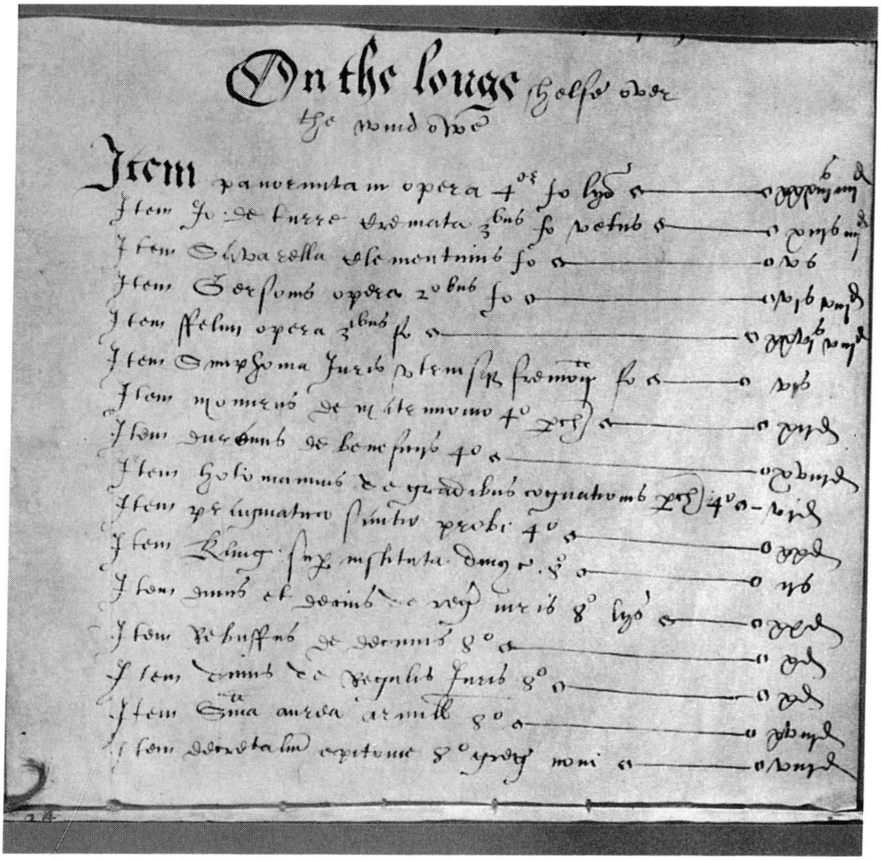
On the longe shelfe over the windowe

Item

Fig. 8 Legal texts in Andrew Perne's library at his death in 1589 (UA Prob. M.1)

which before the end of the sixteenth century had passed into collections of one sort or another. The Cambridge booklists published last year by my friend Elisabeth Leedham-Green allow one to see something of the scope and range of the trade.[14] Nothing is more impressive in her volumes than the inventory of Andrew Perne (164) Master of Peterhouse and Dean of Ely, where some thirty-two specifically canonistic texts (numbers 2413 to 2445) are listed as being 'on the longe shelfe over the windowe in the studdy'. Of these, fourteen are now in Peterhouse Library. None of the Perne books is particularly unusual so far as I can see: there are just a great many of them. Thirty other inventories made between 1542 and 1596 have one or more legal texts, and of these nine have considerable accumulations.

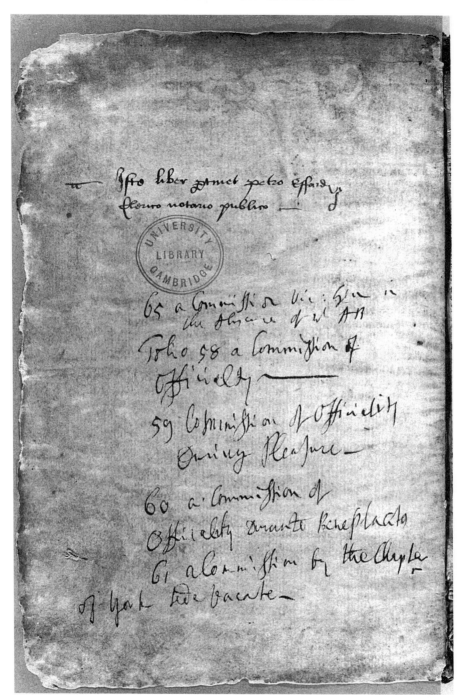

Fig. 9a Signatures of former owners in a York formulary
(ULC Add. ms. 3115)

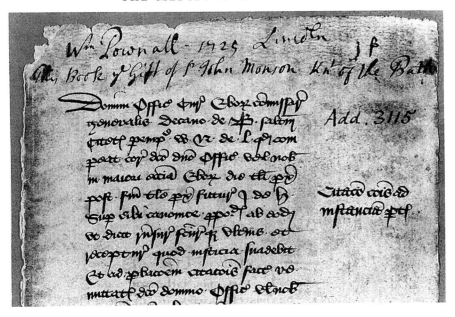

Fig. 9b   Signatures of former owners in a York formulary
(ULC Add. ms. 3115)

Among these nine testators are predictably Thomas Ithell, John
Johnson, and Benedict Thorowgood, who were all officials of the
consistory of Ely. The books owned by the smaller testators are for the
most part Gratian, the decretals, and Lyndwode, varied by Panormita-
nus, Dinus' *de regulis*, Durandus' Speculum and the *Summa Raymundi*.
The longer lists have all of these, as well as 'margarita' (Innocent IV),
Socinus' *de regulis iuris* (1524), a Lyndwode Englished, Baldus de
Ubaldinis on the decretals (1551–85), Lancelotto's *Institutiones iuris
canonici* (1556–87), the Archdeacon on the decretum (1508–77),
Dominicus a Sancto Geminiano on the Sext (1514–78), Brixiensis'
Repertorium, and Hostiensis' *Lectura* (1512). One or two mentions of
books of forms, or notarial acts, occur, but only Benedict Thorowgood, a fellow of Trinity Hall, in 1596 indicated that he was himself a
practitioner of the law by the bequests in his will to his pupil John
Gibson (who had written them) of his tables of the Institutes, and other
collections concerning matrimony, tithes, and legacies, as well as the
two paper books in folio in which were written acts and exhibits
concerning the ecclesiastical courts, besides *Decisiones Rotae* which
were to be given to William Nightingale. John Wyer LL B also of
Trinity Hall, and essentially a civil lawyer, who died in 1556, had a *liber*

scriptus de instrumentis as well as *Decisiones Rotae*. Of this last four examples occur in all.

A privately collected library intended for the use of clergy and inhabitants of the town of Grantham, and founded by Francis Trigge, rector of Welbourne in 1598, has recently been catalogued afresh.[15] It includes several works very similar to those known from Cambridge, though, for the most part, of earlier editions. The *Decretum Aureum* and 'margarita' is of the 1505 edition, the decretal with Bernard and Martianus of Paris 1514, De Milis' *Repertorium* (Basle 1488), Durandus' *Rationale* (Lyons 1499). This has suggested, plausibly enough I suspect, to the compiler of the catalogue that the books were 'bought cheaply enough, without discrimination', and were of only marginal interest to the proposed users. However this may be, a library also designed for use by the clergy and established at Buckden Palace by Bishop William Wake about 1709 (its remnants formed the Huntingdon Archdeaconry library now deposited in the Cambridge University Library) seems to have had a much more immediately practical purpose. It includes Lyndwode of course, a late edition of Swinburne, texts of the decretals and Sext printed at Tournai in 1620–1, Clerke's *Praxis* and Conset's *Practice of the spiritual or ecclesiastical courts*, all plainly intended to be consulted and used.

A quite different and much more profuse collection of law texts had been assembled by Dr Richard Holdworth, master of Emmanuel (dispossessed in 1649) and was bequeathed by him to the University Library on conditions with which I need scarcely trouble the present audience. The *libri juridici* in folio, quarto, and octavo fill thirteen pages of the catalogue. They are, of course, partly civil law texts, with a few works on the common law, and a number of canon law books. These range from early copies of the decretum, Hostiensis, and Bernardus to Richard Cosin's *Tabula* and John Selden's *De successionibus*, though not his *History of Tythes*. The fact that Holdsworth could collect such varied works, without reference to their usefulness, may perhaps reflect only his antiquarian instincts, but it may equally suggest that such works were thought of by himself and his contemporaries as useful to the academic community.[16]

In the first half of the seventeenth century the readers and quoters of the canon law in England seem to have had a purely polemical purpose, and were essentially concerned with the relations between the church courts and the common law. Richard Cosin, for instance was absorbed by such considerations in his *Apologie of and for sundrie proceedings by*

Juridici fol.   133.

Budæus in Pandectas Basil. 1557.
Bassardi Jus Civil. Lugd. 1560
Contarini Codex Juris Civilis 1602
Sigonius de Jure Romano Hannov. 1609.
Brunus de Legationibus Moguntiæ 1548
   De Seditionibus ibid. 1550
Tractatus Variorum de Dote Franc. 1586
Meßiæ Lacomiinus Hispali 1559
Codex Legum Antiquarum Franc. 1613
Geschmÿ Constitutionis Caroli 5ti Hannov. 1614
De Cambariis Tractatus Clausularum Get 1578
Tabula in Aretin. Venet. 1509.
Oldendorpius de Copia Verborum Col. 1532.
De Turrecremata Opa. 3 Vols 1548
Bertachinus 3 Vols Venet. 1519
Regulæ Juris Civ. et Pontificij 2 Vols Lugd. 1579.
Boutie sup Decretalia 2 Vols ibid. 1498.
Imola sup Decretal. 4 Vols ibid. 1525.
Panormitanus sup Decret. 5 Vols ibid
Richardi Gloßa sup Decret. Sexto Parif. 1535
Innocentius sup Decretalia Aug. Taurin. 1581
Idk 1525.
Baldus sup Decretalia Lugd. 1551
Zabarella sup 3tio Decret. ibid. 1517
Geminianus sup 6to Decret.
Sandeus sup Decretalia 2 Vols Lugd. 1555.
Idk 2 Vols 1529.
Marianus Socinus sup Decretalia Lugd. 1533.
De Butrio in Decretal. 3 Vols ibid. 1532.
Hostiensis sup Decretal. 2 Vols Parif. 1512
Ejusd Summa Aurea Basil. 1573.
Bernardus sup Decretalia Argent. 1498
Abbas sup Decretalia
Andreæ sup Decretal. 2 Vols Venet. 1504
Petrus de Anchorano sup Decretal. 3 Vols Lugd.
Archidiaconus sup Sexto Decretal. Venet. 1501
Imola sup Clementinis 1539
De Roselis de Potestate Papæ Col. 1497.

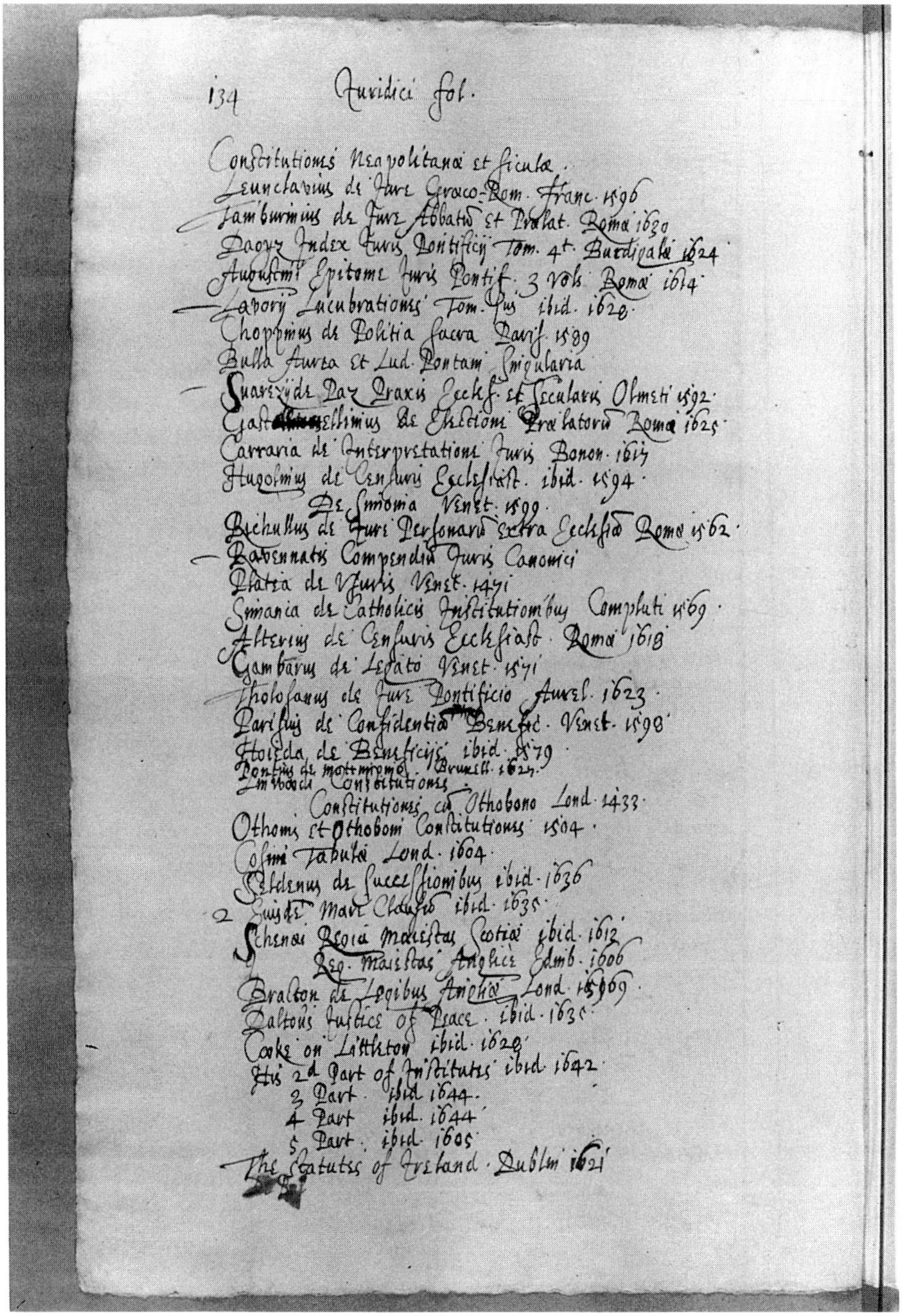

134 Juridici fol.

Constitutiones Neapolitanae et Siculae.
Leunclavius de Iure Graeco-Rom. Franc. 1596
Tamburinus de Iure Abbatum et Praelat. Romae 1630
Daoyz Index Iuris Pontificij Tom. 4t. Burdigalae 1624
Augustini Epitome Iuris Pontif. 3 vols Romae 1614
Zavory Lucubrationes Tom. ... ibid. 1620.
Choppinus de Politia Sacra Parij. 1589
Bulla Aurea et Lud. Pontani Singularia
Suarezij de Pace Praxis Ecclesf. et Secularis Olmeti 1592.
Castellinus de Electione Praelatorum Romae 1625.
Carraria de Interpretatione Iuris Bonon. 1617
Hugolinus de Censuris Ecclesiast. ibid. 1594.
De Simonia Venet. 1599.
Richellus de Iure Personarum extra Ecclesiam Romae 1562.
Ravennatis Compendium Iuris Canonici
Platea de Usuris Venet. 1471
Simancha de Catholicis Institutionibus Compluti 1569.
Alterius de Censuris Ecclesiast. Romae 1618
Gambarus de Legato Venet. 1571
Tholosanus de Iure Pontificio Aurel. 1623.
Parisius de Confidentia Benefic. Venet. 1598
Hoieda de Beneficijs ibid. 1579.
Pontius de matrimonio Bruxell. 1624.
Lyndwoodi Constitutiones
Constitutiones cum Othobono Lond. 1433.
Othonis et Othoboni Constitutiones 1504.
Cosini Tabulae Lond. 1604.
Seldenus de Successionibus ibid. 1636
2 Eiusdem Mare Clausum ibid. 1635.
Skenaei Regia maiestas Scotiae ibid. 1613
Reg. maiestas Angliae Edinb. 1606
Bracton de Legibus Angliae Lond. 1569.
Daltons Iustice of Peace. ibid. 1630.
Coke on Littleton ibid. 1629
His 2d Part of Institutes ibid. 1642.
3 Part. ibid. 1644.
4 Part ibid. 1644.
5 Part. ibid. 1605.
The Statutes of Ireland. Dublin 1621

Figs. 10a–b Law texts in the library of Dr Richard Holdsworth, master of Emmanuel College 1590–1649 (ULC ms. Ff. 4.27)

Jurisdiction ecclesiasticall of late times by some challenged and also diversely by them impugned, 1593. John Selden, primarily a common lawyer, and a Parliamentarian yet also a devoted antiquarian, published in 1618 a *History of Tythes* which was suppressed by the Court of High Commission. In the introduction or preface he was at pains to examine, as he says, the canon law, and to declare that custom in all countries has modified the requirements of the canon law, 'as you shall see in Lindwood, who knew both the general practice here and the canons and often also teaches their difference in other cases'. He goes on to demonstrate that:

the canonist, and more properly now, the civilian, knows nothing of tithes. What in all his Decrees Decretals and Extravagants though he joins many armies of his doctors, directs him to the practice of the Jews, Gentiles or Christians? Where shall the Canonist Civilian or Divine in the course of their proper study find the many secular laws made in the behalf of the clergy for tythes?

This demonstration, unpalatable as it was to be found by the church authorities, was nevertheless based on sound reading, partly in the library of Sir Robert Cotton. Selden's fourteenth chapter 'Of the Jurisdiction over tythes' parades his authorities against the church courts, and this was paralleled by the writings of Spelman and Prynne, who certainly read the canon law in order to be able to oppose it. Selden's mention of the Cottonian library, and its usefulness for his studies, as well as his own collections of the materials of medieval history, are an appropriate prelude to the renewed flowering of English medieval scholarship in the later seventeenth century so ably described by David Douglas.[17] Here the study of the medieval canon law had its own important place, the effects of which can still be felt today.

The Restoration of Charles II heralded the ascendancy in the church of a group of scholars and divines who might appropriately be named, in contrast with the puritans, a high-church party. The church courts re-appeared, though not the High Commission, and fresh impetus seems to have been given to the study and application of the canon law. So far as the universities are concerned it is clear that Oxford was the centre of activity and it is not surprising that there was a renewed demand for an edition of Lyndwode's *Provinciale*, which had not been reprinted since 1560, and may well now have been very scarce. The answer to this was the abbreviated version edited in 1664 by Dr Robert Sharrock of New College, and printed by Henry Hall, the University Printer. This neat little volume includes Lyndwode's whole text, based on the Oxford Badius edition, and the legatine constitutions, but prints only an abbreviated version of the gloss. The publisher was Richard Devis. It is a useful publication, as I have known since 1949, when my own copy was bought for fifteen shillings, but it was plainly not complete, nor grand enough for some readers. The result was the appearance in 1679 of the great Oxford volume, produced during Dr Fell's time as University Printer, and universally respected as the best available edition. It was, like Sharrock's, based on the Badius text of 1506, but this time reproducing in small type, around the main entries, the entire text of the gloss. Its editor is nowhere mentioned and nothing seems to be recoverable about the background to the undertaking. It was thought of as an event of some importance and as Madan pointed out 'had the unusual distinction of being advertised in the *London Gazette* of 30 Jan.–3 Feb. 1678/9'.[18]

Meanwhile there had been going on a sort of learned ferment about the origins of the English church, in which the leading figures were James Ussher, William Lloyd, and Edward Stillingfleet. The latter, a royal chaplain who was later to be bishop of Worcester, was a remarkable man and a remarkable scholar, who was, in his early days, reported by Samuel Pepys to be thought 'the ablest young man to preach the gospel of any since the Apostles' and who had published in 1665, *Origines Sacre*. He followed this in 1684 with *Origines Britannice* which discussed the beginnings of the British Church. Stillingfleet was, in general, moderate in his claims about the church and its privileges, as he demonstrates in 1698 in his defence in *Ecclesiastical causes* of the duties and rights of parochial clergy against the upholders of parochial discipline:

Thus the consistory court was first established as a distinct court from the county court . . . and those who object to the reasonableness of the method of proceeding in these courts must reflect upon some of the wisest nations in the world, who have gone upon the same grounds in all that, have received the Civil law and upon some of the greatest courts at this time in the kingdom as the Chancery and Admiralty which go by the same fundamental rules.

It is scarcely surprising to learn that Stillingfleet was a collector of books and manuscripts and that after his death his collection was sufficiently important to attract the attention of Edward Harley, in whose library it now appears as BL Harleian mss. 665 to 904, 939 to 951, 965 to 1038, and of course includes several of the formularies which are of importance to the present study.

Stillingfleet was a contemporary of the ardent spirits and close learning of the non-juring clergy, who declined to recognise the

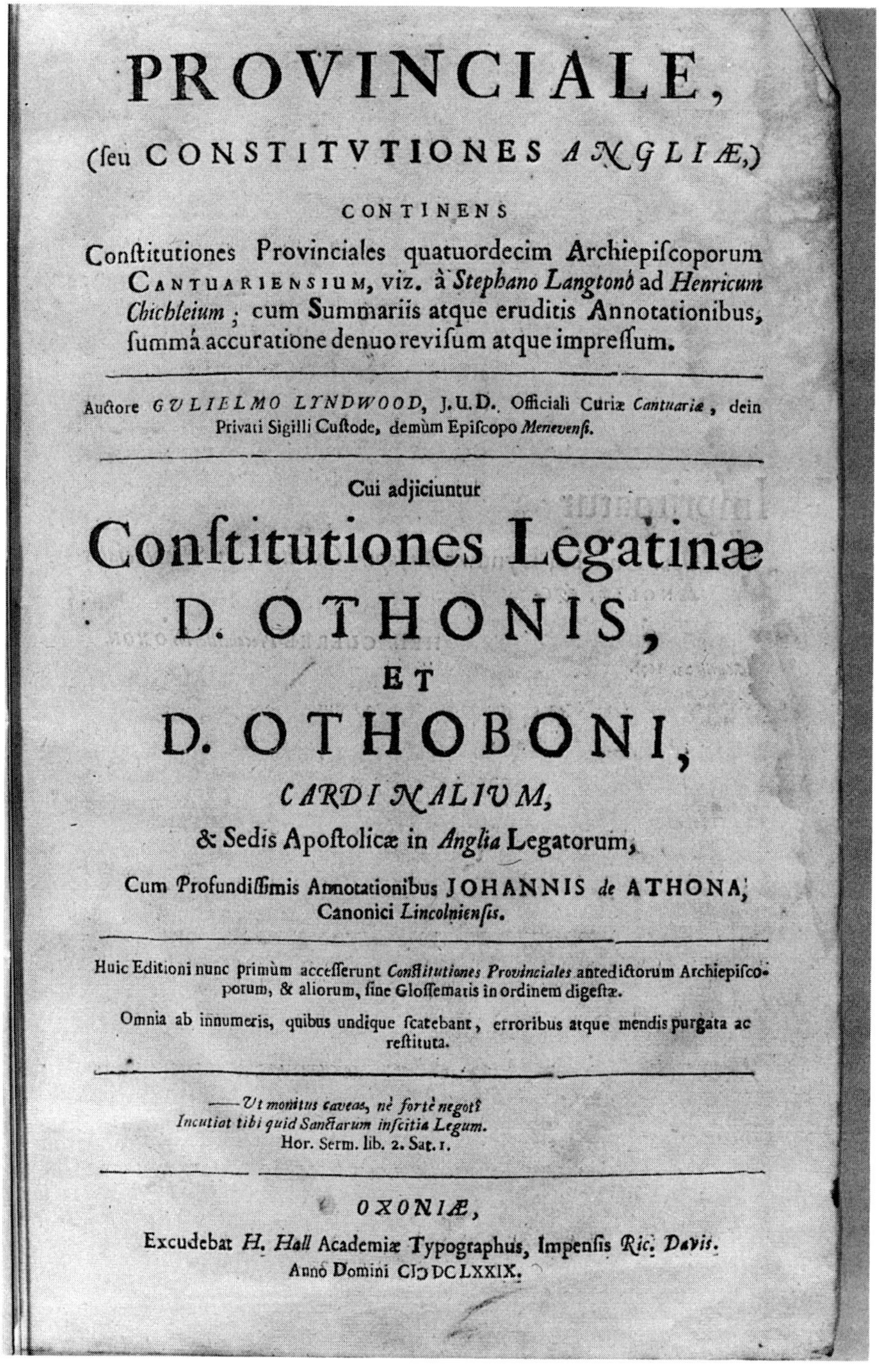

PROVINCIALE,

(seu CONSTITVTIONES ANGLIÆ,)

CONTINENS

Conſtitutiones Provinciales quatuordecim Archiepiſcoporum CANTUARIENSIUM, viz. à *Stephano Langtonò* ad *Henricum Chichleium* ; cum Summariis atque eruditis Annotationibus, ſummâ accuratione denuo reviſum atque impreſſum.

Auctore *GVLIELMO LYNDWOOD*, J.U.D. Officiali Curiæ *Cantuariæ* , dein Privati Sigilli Cuſtode, demùm Epiſcopo *Menevenſi.*

Cui adjiciuntur

Conſtitutiones Legatinæ
D. OTHONIS,
ET
D. OTHOBONI,

CARDINALIVM,

& Sedis Apoſtolicæ in *Anglia* Legatorum,

Cum Profundiſſimis Annotationibus JOHANNIS de ATHONA, Canonici *Lincolnienſis.*

Huic Editioni nunc primùm acceſſerunt *Conſtitutiones Provinciales* antedictorum Archiepiſcoporum, & aliorum, ſine Gloſſematis in ordinem digeſtæ.

Omnia ab innumeris, quibus undique ſcatebant, erroribus atque mendis purgata ac reſtituta.

——*Vt monitus caveas, nè fortè negotî Incutiat tibi quid Sanctarum inſcitia Legum.* Hor. Serm. lib. 2. Sat. 1.

OXONIÆ,

Excudebat *H. Hall* Academiæ Typographus, Impenſis *Ric. Davis.* Anno Domini CIƆ DC LXXIX.

Fig. 11 W. Lyndewode, *'Provinciale' with provincial and legatine constitutions*, Oxford 1679

revolution inaugurated by the accession of William III and Mary II, and who are perhaps best represented here in Cambridge by the scholarly activities of Thomas Baker. The non-jurors seem, surprisingly enough, to have taken no interest in the investigation of church courts, and of parochial antiquities. It is fair to point out that they were closely observant of the forms at least of ecclesiastical law, and that the great Anglo-Saxon scholar, George Hickes, who was one of the most important of their number, in protesting against his own deprivation of the deanery of Worcester in 1690, used the style more common in an appeal to Arches: 'I the said George Hickes do hereby publickly protest and declare that I do claim legal right . . .'[19]

Ecclesiastical jurisdiction was however much more the province of a group of Oxford scholars which centred on the Queen's College, and which included White Kennett, William Nicolson, William Wake, Edmund Gibson, and Thomas Tanner.[20] These men, who were to be in the first thirty years of the eighteenth century the Whig church leaders most closely concerned in a struggle to retain the powers of convocation, were also the leading medieval scholars of their time. Among their works William Wake's study of synodical government, *The state of the church and clergy of England*, 1703, if it did not go directly into the state of ecclesiastical law, certainly gave rise to the publication by David Wilkins, beginning in 1737 of *Concilia Magne Brittanie*, a collection of texts of the English church councils.[21] I have not time to spend on this great project, for what most directly concerns us here is the work of another of the group, Edmund Gibson, bishop successively of Lincoln and London, who in 1713 produced, after a long brooding, as Douglas says, on ecclesiastical laws, *Codex iuris ecclesiastici Anglicani, or the statutes, constitutions, canons, rubrics, and articles of the Church of England*. Gibson began the work with a letter to Archbishop Tenison in which he set out clearly his purpose, which was to 'state the rules by which clergy and laity are to walk so as to impose regularity and discipline in the church'. He produced an exhaustingly thorough (and heavy) work of 1,291 pages, in which, wherever it is appropriate, the constitutions of the medieval church, and their reinforcement by statute law, are clearly set out, with a long appendix of related documents.

Title xxxvi, Of residence, begins for example, with Cardinal Otto's constitution of 1237, followed by Archbishop Pecham's statute concerning the provision of hospitality on behalf of non-residents and continues with a royal statute of 9 Edward IIc.8, concerning the correction by ordinaries of royal clerks following the King's service.

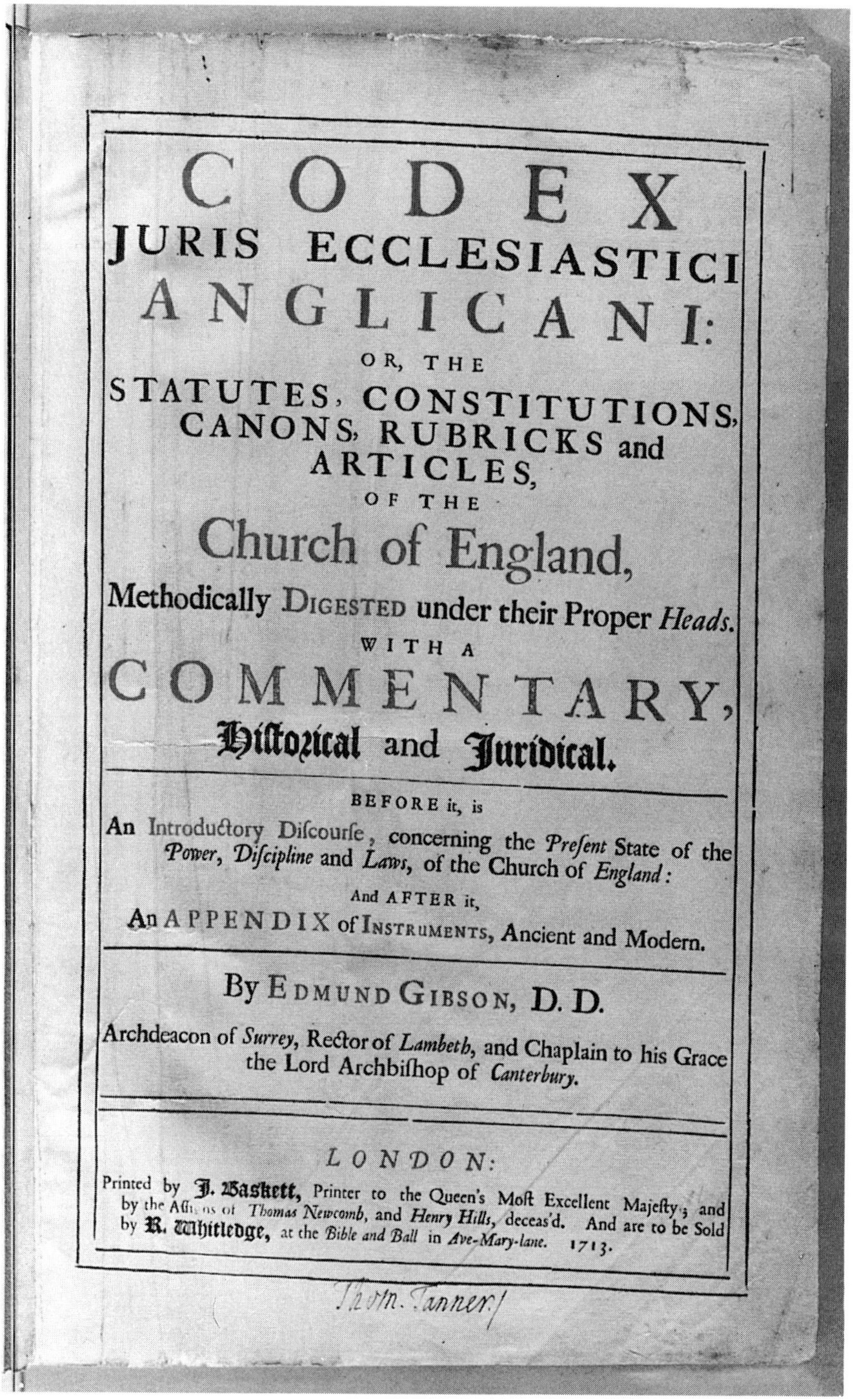

CODEX
JURIS ECCLESIASTICI
ANGLICANI:
OR, THE
STATUTES, CONSTITUTIONS, CANONS, RUBRICKS and ARTICLES,
OF THE
Church of England,
Methodically DIGESTED under their Proper *Heads.*
WITH A
COMMENTARY,
Historical and Juridical.

BEFORE it, is
An Introductory Discourse, concerning the *Present* State of the *Power, Discipline* and *Laws*, of the Church of *England*:
And AFTER it,
An APPENDIX of INSTRUMENTS, Ancient and Modern.

By EDMUND GIBSON, D. D.
Archdeacon of *Surrey*, Rector of *Lambeth*, and Chaplain to his Grace the Lord Archbishop of *Canterbury*.

LONDON:
Printed by J. Baskett, Printer to the Queen's Most Excellent Majesty; and by the Assigns of *Thomas Newcomb*, and *Henry Hills*, deceas'd. And are to be Sold by R. Whitledge, at the *Bible and Ball* in *Ave-Mary-lane*. 1713.

Thom. Tanner.

Fig. 12 Edmund Gibson, *Codex iuris ecclesiastici*, London 1713, showing signature of Thomas Tanner, who annotated this copy freely

The second chapter The Residence of vicars, is made up entirely of the canons on this subject of Langton Otto and Ottobuono.

This work is still of use to the modern scholar, a point on which Professor Cheney did not agree with me, and while it shows no direct evidence of a study of the *Corpus iuris canonici*, it nevertheless marks an important stage in the adaptation of the medieval canon law to the needs of the church of his time. Stubbs was to hail Gibson as a great canonist and to say of the whole of this group of scholars 'the very dust of their writings is gold'.

The *Codex* was thought of by Tory churchmen, as Professor Sykes pointed out, as a party book, and it attracted much unfavourable attention before it was eventually accepted by convocation and I cannot end this section better than by quoting a squib which Sykes prints:

> But for the standard of New Light
> Consult the Codex day and night
> Which shews the genius of the Priest
> Who like a true Church Alchymist
> Can from each *caput mortuum* squeeze
> Religion's culinary fees.
> *Dr Codex's Fifth Pastoral*, T. Cooper, 1734[22]

While antiquarians and controversialists were collecting canon law commentaries from the past (and I am aware that I have left a large field here only partly explored), the civil law courts, now including those of the church, continued to exist, to employ proctors, advocates, and judges, to hear contentious causes, especially those concerning tithe, church rate, the appropriation of pews, and, of course, matrimony and testaments. The disciplinary activities had declined, especially after 1688, but there was increased activity in some areas where members of the Society of Friends were prosecuted for failing to pay tithe and church rates. In the populous districts of the west midlands and suburban London inhabitants of 'new' areas living far from their parish churches, and frequently unprovided with their own place of worship, declined to recognise their duty to pay for the upkeep and repair of the mother church. Many such cases went on appeal to Arches or to the York courts, and so generated an immense amount of business. Miss Doreen Slatter has admirably described this time of increased activity in the Court of Arches, and Dickens' perception of it, drawn partly from his own experiences as a law clerk, and partly from the sort of investigative journalism he practised for

Household Words, are best seen in David Copperfield's life as an articled clerk in a proctor's office in Doctors' Commons. On his first visit you remember David saw:

a great many bundles of papers, some indorsed as allegations, and some (to my surprise) as libels, and some as being in the consistory court, some in the Arches court, some in the Prerogative court, some in the Admiralty court, and some in the Delegates court . . . Besides these there were sundry immense manuscript books of evidence taken on affidavit, strongly bound and tied together in massive sets a set to each cause, as if every cause were a history in ten or twenty volumes.[23]

The nineteenth century saw a renewed ferment in the English church in which inevitably the study of canon law had its place, though less markedly, perhaps, than that of the fathers of the church. Certainly some of the leaders of the Oxford Movement paid lip-service to the importance of church law, though how much most of them knew of it outside the provisions concerning ritual, I am not entirely clear. Robert and Samuel Wilberforce and Henry Manning, each of them new archdeacons in the early forties, had called for a renewed use of spiritual courts as engines of discipline, and Robert Wilberforce had in fact published a tract, based on his own visitation charge of 1843, on *Church courts and church discipline*.[24] A similar preoccupation was echoed by William Hale Hale, archdeacon of London, in a far more scholarly manner, in the extracts from church court records illustrative of the discipline of the Church of England from 1475 to 1640, which he published under the title *A series of precedents and proceedings in criminal causes* in 1847. Hale prefaced his work with an introductory essay which is of great interest for our study. He advanced the theory that the ecclesiastical courts were, from a period at least as early as the reign of Canute, instruments authorised by the state to take charge of public morals and to punish those who offended against the law of God. Hale found it a little difficult to explain the reliance of the post-conquest church courts on Rome, and makes great play with the effect of these constant appeals on the procedure of the courts. Yet, he says, the true judicial authority was, and continued to be, native, and vested in the bishop as ordinary, and his delegate, and later, colleague, the archdeacon. To fortify this position he surprisingly cites a continental work of law by Van Espen, which appeared at Louvain in 1753, he mentions Athon and Lyndwode, and ends with a re-assertion that after 1535 it was 'the papal canon law and not the Anglican canon law' which came to an end.

At almost the same time as Hale's challenge was issued, William

Maskell, an extreme high churchman who subsequently migrated to Rome, and was earlier to be prominent as a supporter of the attempts of his diocesan Henry Philpotts of Exeter to exclude G.C. Gorham from a cure because of his Calvinistic views on baptismal regeneration, began to publish an important series of liturgical studies. I mention him chiefly because I know that he had owned a copy of Hostiensis' *Summa aurea* which was eventually acquired by the chancellor of Ely, J.K. Brunel. Another writer of this period who betrays equal knowledge of the antiquities of ecclesiastical jurisdiction is William Dansey, who in 1834 published his first edition of *Horae Decanicae Rurales*. Dansey went back to the history of the early church to find the origins of the office of rural dean, and like his contemporaries cites Van Espen. He also quotes the Fourth Lateran Council, Athon, and Lyndwode, and, very extensively, Stubbs' golden group of Inett, White Kennett and Gibson himself.

The struggle to revive convocation in the forties and early fifties, which ended in success in 1852, while leading to no such outburst of scholarly activity as accompanied the disputes of 150 years before, had its influence on the reading and study of those most deeply concerned. Of these no doubt Christopher Wordsworth, bishop of Lincoln, and his son John, bishop of Salisbury, are the most conspicuous. Meanwhile some of the strongholds of the canon law had in fact been swept away by the removal from ecclesiastical hands of jurisdiction over probate in 1857, by which Act the college of Doctors' Commons was also dissolved.[25] The original library of the college, as well as most of the records of the court of Arches, had perished in 1666, but by the time the institution was dissolved a very large accumulation of books had been gathered in the new building put up after the fire, and was now sold at auction. These acts paved the way during the next twenty years for the preliminaries of the Ecclesiastical Courts Commission, which reported in 1883. A number of the civilians and clergy professionally involved in the discussions were concerned about the historical background of jurisdiction and of these James Kingdom Brunel, the son and grandson of civil engineers, was particularly distinguished. As chancellor of the diocese of Ely, he monitored the meetings and reports of a series of royal commissions, but, more importantly, he accumulated a library of legal authorities which he bestowed on the bishops of Ely in perpetuity. The books he bequeathed, not all of which have survived, were placed at some point with the diocesan records, and came with them to the University

Library in 1962. I have never seen a list of the original collection as it went to Ely, but it still includes a 1679 *Provinciale*, the copy of Hostiensis I mentioned before, a *Corpus iuris canonici* published at Lyons in 1671, several collections of early councils one of which was bought in from St Maur, and, you will not be surprised to hear, Van Espen. Brunel not only bought the volumes, but used them and they contain a number of annotations on slips of paper on such matters as institution.

A far more important figure in the discussion of ecclesiastical courts was, however, the historian William Stubbs, who, as the contributor of a long historical introduction to the Royal Commission's report, brought into public view the studies with which we have been concerned during the last fortnight. It is neither fashionable, nor, indeed, consonant with the evidence we now have, to accept Stubbs' views on the origin and nature of the post-Reformation ecclesiastical jurisdiction in England, yet no one can deny the merits of his knowledge, and the wide range of his survey. The editor of Stubbs' letters, W.H. Hutton, declared categorically that his most eminent public service was this contribution to the work of the Royal Commission: 'nothing in our generation has done more to impress upon the public the true position and claims of the Church of England than these lucid and exhaustive summaries'. Hutton also printed a letter of Lord Bryce declaring that Gladstone, whose politics were not those of Stubbs, had stated that one of his reasons for giving a bishopric to Stubbs was the importance Stubbs attached to ecclesiastical law and custom.[25] Stubbs' contribution to the study of the canon law was brought home, as it were, by his two professorial lectures on the subject which were reprinted in *Seventeen lectures on the study of medieval and modern history*, the first edition of which appeared from Oxford in 1886. By these lectures, whether we agree with his interpretations or not, he brought the study of the canon law into the field of medieval scholarship and opened the way for Maitland's devastating series of essays, re-published as *The Roman canon law in the Church of England*, which appeared in 1898, for Z.N. Brooke's *English church and the papacy* (1931), and for all that some of us are still doing. Stubbs might be blamed for a good deal, you might say.

Hastings Rashdall, the historian of the medieval universities, once wrote that the intensive study of the canon law was a disaster to the church.[26] Taken out of context (for he went on to say that the lawyers were always a conservative force, hostile to reform) this is a statement with which, though it is no part of my brief to discuss it here, I hope you will not agree. The students and practitioners of the canon law at its height, about 1400 say, were men whose subtle judgments and refined expertise lifted them above mere expediency, and whose achievement produced at best the sort of seemliness and order which can never be undesirable. What the successors of these matured scholars made of it is of course predictable, but that we are not going to discuss here.

I began these lectures with a reminder to you of the scholar whom I follow, however humbly, but I cannot end them without a brief reference to Samuel Sandars, by whose liberality the whole series was founded in 1894, and whom we annually commemorate. In the words of the university's Commemoration of Benefactors: 'to the perpetuating of his memory and the testifying of our own thankfulness

TE DEUM LAUDAMUS'.

Notes

I. THE TEACHING AND STUDY OF THE CANON LAW IN THE LATER MIDDLE AGES

1 QCO ms. 54, f. 93.
2 *VCH Cambridge*, vol. III, ed. J.P.C. Roach, 1959, p. 174.
3 37 Henry VIII, c. 17.
4 *Registrum S. de Gandavo*, ed. C.T. Flower, C&YS, vol. XL, 1934, pp. 318–20.
5 For these texts consult *Corpus iuris canonici*, ed. A. Friedburg, 2 vols., Leipzig 1879–81.
6 C.R. Cheney, *English Synodalia of the thirteenth century*, Oxford 1941; F.M. Powicke and C.R. Cheney, *Councils and Synods*, no. 2, 2 vols., Oxford 1964.
7 Bishop Lisle of Ely granted to Trinity Hall, in support of its studies in canon law, the endowments of the two rectories of St John and St Edward, Cambridge, *Warren's Book*, ed. A.W.W. Dale, Cambridge 1911, p. 55.
8 C.R. Cheney, *Notaries Public in England in the thirteenth and fourteenth centuries*, Oxford 1972.
9 M.B. Hackett, *The original statutes of Cambridge university*, Cambridge 1970, p. 69.
10 L.E. Boyle, 'The canon law before 1381', in *The history of the university of Oxford*, ed. J.I. Catto, vol. I, Oxford 1984, pp. 531–64.
11 *Statuta antiqua in ordinem redacta*, in *Documents*, vol. I; statutes 93, 99, 103, 104, 105, 122, 131, 151, all relate to the study of canon law.
12 QCO ms. 54, f. 104.
13 G&C ms. 483/479.
14 UA Com ct. 1/10, 1/11.
15 QCO ms. 54, f. 93v.
16 L.E. Boyle, 'The constitution *cum ex eo* of Boniface viii', reprinted in *Pastoral care, clerical education and canon law 1200–1400*, Variorum Reprints, London 1981, pp. 263–302.
17 Mrs A.H. Lloyd, 'Notes on Cambridge clerks petitioning for benefices 1370–1399', *BIHR* 20 (1944–5), 75–96, 192–211; E.F. Jacob, 'Petitions for benefices from English universities during the Great Schism', in his *Essays in the conciliar epoch*, 3rd edn, Manchester 1963, pp. 223–39. The original rolls of petitions are in UA Luard 82*.
18 S.M. Leathes, *Grace Book A*, Luard memorial series 1, Cambridge 1897, p. 29.
19 QCO ms. 54, ff. 112r and v; F.D. Logan, 'The Cambridge law faculty', *Bulletin of Medieval Canon Law*, n.s. 15 (1985), 117–18.
20 UA Luard 16.
21 CCC The White register, plan of the Common Schools, reproduced by R. Willis and J.W. Clark, *Architectural history of the university of Cambridge*, 3 vols., Cambridge 1886, vol. III, p. 5.

22 EDR K 1–26 (court papers) *passim*; H.P. Stokes, *The medieval hostels of the university of Cambridge*, CAS 8vo series, no. 49, 1924.

23 UA Coll. Admin. 4, f. 44v; see also figure 2 above.

24 *BRUC*, pp. 311–12; *Proceedings of the Archaeological Institute at Lincoln 1848*, London 1850, pp. 312–27; A. Gibbons, *Early Lincoln Wills*, privately printed, Lincoln 1888, pp. 67–9.

25 H. Bradshaw, *Collected Papers*, Cambridge 1889, pp. 16–54, 186–7.

26 *Documents*, vol. II, pp. 22, 56, 69, 159; A.B. Cobban, *The King's Hall within the university of Cambridge in the later middle ages*, Cambridge 1969, pp. 255–93; *The King's scholars and King's Hall* (no author), privately printed, Cambridge 1917, p. 49.

27 C.N.L. Brooke, *A history of Gonville and Caius College*, Woodbridge, Suffolk 1985, pp. 1–19.

28 *Documents*, vol. II, pp. 417–18, 424, 432.

29 Ibid. pp. 452, 548; King's College Mundum book v, ff. 67v, 124r and v. I am grateful to my husband for these references.

30 J.D. Twigg, *A history of Queens' College Cambridge*, Woodbridge, Suffolk 1987, p. 10; *Documents*, vol. III, pp. 44, 82–3.

31 R. Lovatt, 'The first century of the college library', *Peterhouse Record*, 1983–4, pp. 66–73 and M.R. James, *Catalogue of the manuscripts of Peterhouse*, Cambridge 1899, pp. 22–3, from a 1418 list in the Old Register.

32 Warren's Book, pp. 44–7 and UA Luard 39; see figure 3 above.

33 R.W. Hunt, 'Medieval inventories of Clare College Library', *TCBS*, I (1949–53), 105–25.

34 M.R. James, *Catalogue of the manuscripts of Pembroke College*, Cambridge 1905, pp. xiii, xvi, 15, 79, 161, 176, 178–9.

35 CCC ms. 232, register of Markaunt's benefactions; C.R. Cheney, 'A register of manuscripts borrowed from a college library, 1440–1517', *TCBS* 4 (1988), 103–29.

36 C.E. Sayle, 'The library of King's Hall', *PCAS* 24 (1921–2), 67.

37 Brooke, *Gonville and Caius*, pp. 36–7.

38 Andrew Doket's inventory, in the keeping of the President of Queens' College, ff. 7v and 8, *BRUC*, *passim*.

39 UA Coll. Admin. 2 (the Junior Proctor's book), f. 153v.

40 T.J. Raine, *Testamenta Eboracensia* vol. I, SS 4, 1836; *BRUC*, pp. 421–2.

41 UA CUR 1.2, Aa and 1–54.

42 *BRUC passim*, citing Gibbons, *Early Lincoln wills*, and *Testamenta Eboracensia*, vol. I, pp. 385–9, II, 78.

43 E.S. Leedham-Green, *Books in Cambridge inventories*, 2 vols., Cambridge 1986, pp. xx, 55–7.

44 A. Hamilton Thompson, 'The will of Master William Doune', *Archaeological Journal*, 72 (1915), 233–84.

45 F.C. Hingeston Randolph, *Register of Walter Stapeldon*, London and Exeter 1892, pp. 563–5.

46 W.W. Capes, *Charters and Records of Hereford Cathedral*, Cantelupe Society, Hereford 1980, pp. 260–2.

47 *Testamenta Eboracensia*, vol. IV, pp. 277–82.

48 BL ms. Cotton Vesp. b xi f. 61v.

49 C.L. Feltoe and E.H. Minns, *Vetus Liber Archidiaconi Eliensis*, CAS 8vo no. 48

1917; A Watkin, *Inventory of Church goods temp. Edward* III, Norfolk Record Society, 2 parts 1947; Dorothy M. Owen, 'Two medieval parish books', *Reading Medieval Studies* 11 (1985), 121–32.

50 This is perhaps a confusion with another Dominican of the same name, who was a graduate of Oxford, *BRUC*, p. 96; *BRUO* vol. I, p. 278.

2. CANONISTS AND THEIR CAREERS

1 QCO ms. 54, f. 187v.

2 BL ms. Egerton 2886, ff. 47, 79, 81, 103, 124, 127v.

3 *BRUC*, p. 90; QCO ms. 54, f. 62v.

4 W.T. Mellows, *The last days of Peterborough Monastery*, Northants. Record Society no. 12, 1947, pp. ci and 113.

5 *BRUC*, p. 95.

6 B. Woodcock, *Medieval ecclesiastical courts in the diocese of Canterbury*, Oxford 1952, pp. 42–3; R.L. Storey, *Diocesan administration in the fifteenth century*, Borthwick Paper 16, second edn, York 1972.

7 Register of W. Stapeldon, pp. 115–19.

8 R.M. Haines, *Administration of the diocese of Worcester in the first half of the fourteenth century*, London 1965, pp. 75–140.

9 Dorothy M. Owen, 'An episcopal audience court', *Legal records and the historian*, ed. J.H. Baker, Royal Historical Society Study in history no. 7, London 1978, pp. 140–9.

10 Dorothy M. Owen, *John Lydford's book*, Historical Manuscripts Commission Joint publication 22, Devon and Cornwall Record Society 19, Exeter 1974, pp. 5–11, 15–20.

11 'The Will of Master William Doune'.

12 F.C. Hingeston Randolph, *The register of John de Grandisson*, Exeter 1894, p. 986; C.W. Boase, *Registrum collegii Exoniensis*, Oxford Historical Society, vol. 27, Oxford 1894; Owen, *Lydford*, p. 5.

13 *BRUC*, p. 44; W.H. Bliss, *Calendar of papal petitions*, vol. I, pp. 8–10, 276–7, London 1896; A. Hamilton Thompson, 'William Bateman Bishop of Norwich', *Norfolk Archaeology*, 25 (1935–7), 102–37.

14 H.M. Chew, *Hemingby's Register*, Wiltshire Archaeological Society, Records Branch, vol. XVIII, Devizes 1962, nos. 225, 227–9.

15 Dorothy M. Owen, 'The records of the bishop's official at Ely: specialisation in the English episcopal chancery of the later middle ages', in D.A. Bullough and R.L. Storey, *The study of medieval records*, Oxford 1971, pp. 189–205.

16 C. Johnson, *Registrum Hamonis de Hethe*, C&YS vols. XLVII and XLIX, 1914 and 1948, pp. 911–1043.

17 Dorothy M. Owen, 'Vetus repertorium', *TCBS* 4, 2, (1965), 100–6; G&C mss. 170 and 204; PRO KR Misc books ser. I, vol. XXX, described by Watkin, *Inventory*.

18 VI°, 1.17 c. 7.

19 I was allowed by Professor J.A. Brundage to see the text of a paper he subsequently read to the eighth international conference of medieval canon law held at the university of California, San Diego, in August 1988, on 'The ecclesiastical bar at Ely in the fourteenth century'; for commissary courts, see

C. Morris, 'The commissary of the Bishop in the diocese of Lincoln', *JEH* 10 (1959), 50–65; see also figure 5 above.

20 E.F. Jacob, 'To and from the court of Rome in the early fifteenth century', *Essays in later medieval history*, Manchester 1968, pp. 58–97; P.N.R. Zutshi, 'Proctors acting for English petitioners . . . 1305–78', *JEH*, 35 (1984), 15–29.

21 R.J. Mitchell, 'Engish law students at Bologna in the fifteenth century', *EHR* 51 (1936), 270–87.

22 LAO Lincoln diocesan records, register 12, f. 389; the statutes of the Lincoln consistory were printed by David Wilkins from a New College manuscript in *Concilia magne Britannie et Hibernie*, vol. II, p. 574.

23 *Corpus iuris canonici academici*, ad modum Christoph' Henr' Freiesleben, 2 vols., Cologne, 1773, vol. 2, preface p. ii.

24 L. Lefèbre, 'Procédure', *DDC*, vol. 7, 1965, cols. 285–96.

25 I have discussed this subject in greater detail in 'Ecclesiastical jurisdiction in England', *Studies in Church History*, vol. XI, 1975, pp. 199–222; see also J.D. Mansi, *Sacrorum conciliorum nova et amplissima collectio*, vol. XXII, Rome 1778, cols. 1,022–3. A handlist of the fourteenth-century papers has now appeared, compiled by D.M. Smith, *Borthwick text and calendar*, no. 14, York 1988.

26 York Borthwick Institute, CPF 63.

27 R.W. Hunt, 'A tuitorial appeal in the fourteenth century before the court of Arches', *Transactions of the Historical Society of Lancashire and Cheshire*, vol. CI, 1949, pp. 47–61.

28 Some of the documents in this interesting cause were copied by Lydford (nos. 78–81); the Hereford references are 3170, 3211, 3017–20, 3024–41.

29 A copy of this fragment is in the East Sussex Record Office AMS 2955. I am grateful to Mr Christopher Whittick of that office for drawing my attention to it.

30 *Summa aurea* c. iii, cited by Dr Jane Sayers, *Papal judges delegate in the province of Canterbury 1198–1254*, Oxford, 1971, p. 222, from L. Wahrmund, *Quellen zur Geschichte des Römisch-Kanonischen Processes in Mittelalter*, Innsbruck 1914, vol. II, part 2, pp. 98–9.

31 LAO Lincoln Diocesan Records, Ben 3/78,

32 J.H. Baker, 'Dr. Thomas Fastolf and the history of law reporting', *Cambridge Law Journal*, 45, 1 (March 1986), 84–96.

3. THE CANONIST'S FORMULARIES

1 Published by the Oxfordshire Local History Society on the cover of the annual report for 1976.

2 Cheney, *Notaries public in England*, pp. 10–11 and note 1.

3 J.E. Sayers, 'Canterbury Proctors at the court of *audientia litterarum contradictarum*', *Traditio*, 22 (1966), 311–45 and *Papal judges delegate*, pp. 42–54; F.D. Logan, 'An early thirteenth century papal judges delegate formulary of English origin', *Studia Gratiana*, 14 (1967), 73–87; C.R. Cheney, *English bishops' chanceries 1100–1250*, Manchester 1950, pp. 124–30.

4 B.Z. Kedar, 'Canon law and local practice', *Bulletin of medieval Canon Law*, 2 (1972), 17–32.

5 I.J. Churchill, *Canterbury Administration*, 2 vols., London, 1933, pp. 435–6.

6 'The will of Master William Doune', p. 237.

7 Gibbons, *Early Lincoln wills*, pp. 26–7.
8 Capes, *Charters and records of Hereford Cathedral*, pp. 259–62.
9 E.F. Jacob and H.C. Johnson, *The register of Henry Chichele*, vol. II, Oxford 1938, pp. 163–4.
10 *Testamenta Eboracensia*, vol. II, pp. 78, 90.
11 Jacob, 'To and from the court of Rome', p. 73.
12 I have discussed some Ely examples in 'Why and how? Some thoughts on the cataloguing of ecclesiastical archives', *Journal of the Society of Archivists*, 2, 10 (1964), 467–71.
13 Professor Logan and I are now engaged on the compilation of a list and full description of such documents, which we hope to be able to publish.
14 C.E. and R.C. Wright, *The diary of Humphrey Wanley*, Bibliographical Society, London 1966, p. xix; D.C. Douglas, *English Scholars*, revised edn 1951, p. 25.
15 Owen, *John Lydford's Book*, 1974.
16 'The will of Master William Doune'; H.E. Salter, *Snappe's Formulary and other Records*, Oxford Historical Society, vols. 93, 94, Oxford 1932.
17 E.F. Jacob, *Essays in the Conciliar Epoch*, Manchester 1962, p. 58.
18 'A visitation of the archdeaconry of Totnes in 1342' (*sic*), *EHR*, 101 (1911), 108–24.

4. POST–REFORMATION LITERATURE: COLLECTORS AND PRACTICAL APPLICATIONS

1 This is embodied in the Act of Parliament 25 Henry VIII c. 20.
2 Act of Parliament 37 Henry VIII c. 19.
3 G.I.O. Duncan, *The High Court of Delegates*, Cambridge 1971.
4 R.G. Usher, *The rise and fall of the High Commission*, reprinted 1968; for the Northern Commission see P. Tyler, 'The significance of the ecclesiastical commission at York', *Northern History*, 2 (1967), 27–44.
5 G.D. Squibb, *Doctors' Commons*, Oxford 1977.
6 J.A. Sharpe, *Defamation and sexual slander in early modern England: the Church courts at York*, Borthwick paper no. 58, York 1980.
7 J.D.M. Derrett, *Henry Swinburne, c. 1551–1624, Civil Lawyer of York*, Borthwick paper no. 44, York 1973; J.D.M. Derrett, 'The works of Francis Clerke, proctor', in *Studia et documenta historie et iuris*, 40 (1974).
8 Swinburne, appendix ii, pp. 32–50, where Swinburne's sources demonstrate very clearly the width of his reading; see also figure 7 above.
9 T.F. Barton, *The registrum vagum of Anthony Harison*, Norfolk Record Society, vols. 32 and 33, Norwich 1963, pp. 77–81.
10 As he demonstrates in his compilation on ecclesiastical law which remains in the University Archives: UA Coll. Admin. 29.
11 John Addy, *The diary of Henry Prescott LL B, deputy registrar of Chester diocese*, vol. I, Record Society of Lancashire and Cheshire 127, produced by Alan Sutton of Gloucester, 1987, pp. 15, 24, 34, 37, 173, 224.
12 F.S. Hockaday, 'The consistory court of the diocese of Gloucester', *Transactions of the Bristol and Gloucester Archaeological Society*, 46 (1924), 195–287.
13 P.M. Stewart, *Guide to the records of the Bishop, the Archdeacons of Salisbury and Wiltshire . . .*, Wiltshire County Council, 1973, pp. 84–7; D.M. Smith, *A guide to the archives collections in the Borthwick Institute of Historical Research*, York, 1973;

Dorothy M. Owen, *Ely Records*, Cambridge 1970, pp. 29–34; K. Major, *A hand-list of the records of the Bishop of Lincoln*, Oxford 1953, pp. 338–9.

14 *Books in Cambridge Inventories*, 2 vols. Cambridge 1987, *passim*. See also figure 8 above.

15 J. Glenn/D. Walsh, *Catalogue of the Francis Twigge chained library*, D.S. Brewer, Woodbridge, Suffolk, 1988.

16 The Holdsworth Catalogue is in CUL Ff.4.27; see also figures 10a and 10b above.

17 Douglas, *English Scholars*.

18 F. Madan, *Oxford Books*, vol. III, 1931, no. 3221, pp. 374–5; see also figure 11 above.

19 Douglas, *English Scholars*; R. Latham, *The Shorter Pepys*, London 1985, p. 484.

20 G.V. Bennett, *White Kennett*, London 1957, p. 81; W. Stubbs, *Seventeen lectures on the study of medieval and modern history*, Oxford 1886, p. 331.

21 F.M. Powicke, 'Sir Henry Spelman and the Concilia', British Academy pamphlet, 1930; E.F. Jacob, 'Wilkins' Concilia and the fifteenth century', *TRHS*, 4th series, 15 (1932), 91–131.

22 N. Sykes, *Edmund Gibson Bishop of London, 1669–1748*, Oxford 1926, pp. 64–5 and 70 n. 1; see also figure 12 above.

23 M.D. Slatter, 'The records of the court of Arches', *JEH*, 4 (1954), 139–53; C. Dickens, *David Copperfield*, Harmondsworth 1960, c. xxiii.

24 D. Newsome, *The parting of friends*, London 1966, pp. 255–307.

25 *Report of the commissioners appointed to inquire into the constitution and working of the ecclesiastical courts*, c. 3760, 2 vols., 1883; Stubbs' historical appendices are at vol. I, pp. 21–141; W.H. Hutton, *Letters of William Stubbs*, London 1904, pp. 204–6.

26 H. Rashdall, *The universities of Europe in the middle ages*, ed. F.M. Powicke and A.B. Emden, 3 vols., Oxford, 1936, vol. I, pp. 139–40.

Bibliography of works quoted

MANUSCRIPTS QUOTED EXTENSIVELY

Cambridge CCC ms. 170
           G&C mss. 30, 45, 54, 67, 172, 254, 280, 483
           Pembroke College mss. 165, 188
           Peterhouse mss. 42, 264
           Trinity College mss. 397, 1245
           ULC mss. Dd.10.28, Mm. 4.41, Add. 3115, 3468; UA Coll.
               Admin. 38, 39; EDR D/2/1, F5/32, 33
Oxford   All Souls ms. 182
           New College mss. 182, 192, 197
           QCO ms. 54
London   BL Harleian ms. 862
           PRO KR Misc. bks ser. 1, vol. xxx
Bristol Record Office, 1A/6/1
Devon Record Office, Exeter diocesan records, John Lydford's book
Hereford Cathedral muniments (Syde cause), nos. 1932, 3170, 3210, 3017–41
Kent Archives Office, Rochester Diocesan Records Dr b 010
LAO, Lincoln Diocesan Records Ben 3/78; Form. 23
Northamptonshire Archives Office, Peterborough Diocesan Records Misc. Bk. 1
    (Snappe)
York Borthwick Institute, register 13

WORKS OF CANON LAWYERS, PRE-REFORMATION

Anchorano, Peter of. *In quinque libros decretalium fecundissima commentaria*, 5 vols,
    Bologna 1580–81; *DDC*, vol. VI, pp. 1474–71
Ancona, John of. *DDC*, vol. VI, pp. 87–8
Andreas, John (*c.* 1270–1348). The *novella*, a commentary on decretals and Sext, the
    latter of which became the *glossa ordinaria*; de regulis iuris; *DDC*, vol. VI,
    pp. 89–92
Archdeacon (Guy de Basio, died 1311). Commentary *in Rosario*, on the decretum and
    Sext; *DDC*, vol. V, pp. 1007–8
Baldus (de Ubaldinis, *c.* 1319–1400). *ad tres priores libros decretalium commentaria*, Lyon,
    1585; *DDC*, vol. II, pp. 39–52
Brixiensis (Bartholomew of Brescia, died 1258). *Tractatus universi iuris*, 22 vols. in 28,
    Venice, Franciscus Zitellus, 1584–86; *DDC*, vol. II, pp. 215–17
Bromyerd, Fr. John (died *c.* 1390 or 1413). Distinctiones super certos titulos iuris
    civilis et canonici; *DDC*, vol. VI, pp. 95–6
Dominicus a Sancto Geminiano (died before 1436). *Lectura super sextum decretalium*,
    5 parts, Venice 1476–7 and 1485

Durandus, Gulielmus (Speculator, died 1296). Repertorium; Speculum iudiciale; *DDC*, vol. v, pp. 1014–75

Dyne, John (Dinus Magellanus, died 1313). Engaged on the redaction of the Sext, to which he contributed *titulus de regulis iuris* which forms the concluding section

Faventinus, John (*c.* 1171). summa; *DDC*, vol. vi, pp. 99–102

Hostiensis (Henry of Susa, *c.* 1200–71). Summa copiosa: *Summa aurea*, Venice 1570; *Lectura in quinque libros decretalium*, Venice, 1581; *DDC*, vol. v, pp. 1211–27

Huguccio (of Pisa, died 1210). Taught at Bologna; author of a summa; *DDC*, vol. viii, pp. 1355–62

Imola, John of (*c.* 1376–1436). *Commentaria super tres libros decretalium*, Venice, 1498, 1500; *DDC*, vol. vi, pp. 107–10

Innocent IV, Pope (died 1254). Margarita super decretum; solennis apparatus super quinque libros decretalium

Lancelotto (1522–90). *Institutiones iuris canonici 1556–87*, Perugia 1563, Venice

Ligno, John of (1320–83). Lectura on the Clementines; *DDC*, vol. vi, pp. 111–12

Martiana, Tabula (Martin de Fano, OP, taught at Bologna died *c.* 1275). *DDC*, vol. vi, pp. 836–7

Monachus, John (*c.* 1250–1313). Gloss on decretals and Sext; *DDC*, vol. vi, pp. 111–12

Monte Lauduno, William of (died 1343). Lectura on Clementines, printed in Rouen edition of the Corpus of 1512; *DDC*, vol. vi, pp. 1078–9

Panormitanus (Abbas, Nicholas of Tuda 1386–1445). Commentary on decretum, many printed editions; *DDC*, vol. vi, pp. 1195–1215

Parma, Bernard of (*c.* 1200–1266). Casus super decretales (the glossa ordinaria); *DDC*, vol. ii, pp. 781–2

Penaforte, Reimundus (*c.* 1175–1260). summa de penitentia; summa de matrimonio; *DDC*, vol. vii, pp. 461–4

Ruffinus (died 1192). Summa decretorum; *DDC*, vol. vii, pp. 779–84

Sampson (de calvo monte, *c.* 1310). La lectura on Hostiensis and perhaps a later commentary on the Extravagants; *DDC*, vol. vii, p. 864

Socinus, Mariano (1401–67). de regulis iuris; *DDC*, vol. vii, p. 1063

Summa aurea Armilli, F. Bartholomeus, *Summa que aurea Armilli inscribitur*, Venice, 1550, Lyons, 1596

Trano, Godfrey of (died 1245). Summa on the decretals; *DDC*, vol. v, p. 952

Vankel, John Koelner de (died 1490). *Summarium textuale et conclusiones super Clementinas*, Cologne, Koelhoff, 1484; *DDC*, vol. vi, pp. 127–8

Vincentius Hispanus (died 1248). Gloss on decretals; *DDC*, vol. vii, pp. 1508–8

Zabarella, Franciscus. *Commentarii in Clementinarum volumen*, Venice 1502

WORKS ON CANON LAW, POST-REFORMATION

Ayliffe, John. *Parergon iuris canonici Anglicani or a commentary by way of supplement to the constitutions of the Church of England*, London 1726

Burn, Richard. *Ecclesiastical Law*, 2 vols., London 1763

Clerke, Francis. *Praxis Francisci Clarke, omnibusque in foro ecclesiastico versantur utilis per Thomas Bladen primo in lucem edita*, Dublin 1666

Conset, Henry. *Practice of the spiritual or ecclesiastical courts*, London 1681

Cosin, Richard. *Apologie of and for sundrie proceedings by Jurisdiction ecclesiasticall of late times by some challenged and also diversely by them impugned*, London 1593

Ecclesie anglicane politeia in tabula digesta, London 1604, Oxford 1634 and 1684

Godolphin, John. *Repertorium canonicum or an abridgment of the ecclesiastical law of this realm*, London 1678 and 1680 (two versions)

Dansey, William. *Horae Decanicae Rurales*, 2 vols., London 1834, 1845

Gibson, Edmund. *Codex iuris ecclesiastici Anglicani, or the statutes, constitutions, canons, rubrics, and articles of the Church of England*, 2 vols., London 1713

Hale, William Hale. *A series of precedents and proceedings in criminal causes, 1475–1640, extracted from the act books of ecclesiastical courts in the diocese of London illustrative of the discipline of the Church of England*, London 1847

March, John. *Actions for slander or a methodicall collection under certain grounds of heads of what words are actionable in the law, and what not?* London 1647

Oughton, Thomas. *Ordo iudiciorum sive methodus procedendi in negotiis et litibus in foro ecclesiastico civili*, 2 vols., London 1728, 1 vol., 1738. J.T. Law published a translation of part I: *Forms of ecclesiastical law, or the mode of conducting suits in the consistory courts*, London 1831

Selden, John. *A history of tythes*, London 1618

De successionibus in bonis defuncti seu iure hereditario, London 1631

Stillingfleet, Edward. *Ecclesiastical causes of the duties and rights of parochial clergy against the upholders of parochial discipline*, London 1698

Swinburne, Henry. *Briefe treatise of testamentes and last willes*, London 1590

Van Espen, Z.B. *Ius Ecclesie universum*, 5 vols., Brussels and Paris 1753–68

Wake, William. *The state of the church and clergy of England*, London 1703

Wilberforce, Robert Isaac. *Church courts and church discipline*, London 1843

Wilkins, David. *Concilia Magne Britannie at Hibernie*, 4 vols., London 1737

Index

testaments, viii, 45 (fig. 7), 46, 48, 53

Sykes, Professor Norman, 61

Sympson, Thomas, 49

Tabor, James, 48

Tallington, Lincs., 29

Tanner, Thomas, viii, 59, 60 (fig. 12)

Tapton, Mr Hugh, 5

Tenison, Thomas, archbishop of Canterbury, 59

testamentary matters, litigation on, 46–7

Tetford, Thomas, abbot of Bermondsey, 37

Thompson, A. Hamilton, 35

Thorowgood, Benedict, official of Ely, 52

Thurlby, Thomas, 40

Trano, Godfrey of, commentary on decretals, 11

Trefnant, John, bishop of Hereford, 14, 32

Tregrisiou, Ralph, dean of Exeter, 19, 34

Trigge, Francis, 53

Ubaldinis, Baldus de, commentary on decretals, 11, 52

Ufford, John of, 20

Ussher, James, archbishop of Armagh, 57

Vallensis, Andrew, 13

Vankel, Koelner de, commentary on Clementines, 14

Van Espen, Z. B., *Ius ecclesie universum*, 62–4

Varley, Joan, ix

Vincent, Vincentius Hispanus, gloss on decretals, 11

Waddington, Arthur, schoolmaster of Alford, 14

Wainwright, John, chancellor of the diocese of Chester, 48

Wake, William, bishop of Lincoln and archbishop of Canterbury, 53, 59

Waltham, William of, 11

Welle, Henry, clerk, 32

Welles, Thomas, advocate of consistory of Norwich, 11

Wells, Somerset
cathedral, 28
consistory of, 26

Wenlok, Mr William, 36

West, Nicholas, bishop of Ely, 33

Westminster
archdeaconry of see London, John
monastic liberty of, 22

Whittlesey, William, archbishop of Canterbury, 23

Wickmer, Adam of, examiner general of the courts of Canterbury, 10

Wilberforce
Robert, archdeacon of the East Riding, 62
Samuel, archdeacon of Surrey, bishop of Oxford and Winchester, 62

Wilkins, David, 59

Winchelsey, Robert, archbishop of Canterbury, 1, 31, 39

Windsor, Berks., St George's chapel, 28

Wodestok or Heete, R. of, 16

Woller, Mr Robert, 36

Wolsey, Cardinal Thomas, 17

Woodcock, Brian, 18

Worcester
consistory of, 27
diocese of, 18–9

Wordsworth
Christopher, bishop of Lincoln, 63
John, bishop of Salisbury, 63

Wormenhale, Thomas of, auditor of Arches, official of Ely, 23

Worth, Robert, chancellor of Ely, 8

Wortham, Mr John, rector of Fowlmire, Cambs., 15

Wycliffe, John, 19, 34

Wyer, John, LLB, 52

Wykeham, William of, bishop of Winchester, 34

Wymondham, Norfolk, 37, 48

York
archiepiscopal records, 33